Not Created to Break

A Journey in Search of Hope, Love, and Forgiveness

Alisa D. Boyd

Dr. Jackie S. Henderson
Your Family Research & Publishing
Stone Mountain, Georgia

The following is a true story. However, the name of a few characters, places and events have been changed in order to protect their privacy, and any resemblance to actual persons dead or alive is merely coincidental.

Copyright © 2016 Alisa D. Boyd

All rights reserved.

ISBN-13:978-1511680820

ISBN-10:1511680822

DEDICATION

Inspiration ... I love the Lord because He heard my cry. "... weeping may endure for a night, but joy cometh in the morning" (Psalms 30:5b KJV).

Resting in the presence of The Most High: My maternal grandfather instructed me on how to better sow seeds of goodness so that righteousness may bloom due to my actions. My maternal grandmother showered my life with prayers and blessed me with the knowledge of Christ that it may bring into fruition wisdom. My paternal grandmother came into my life in my late teens and validated my connection to my biological father's bloodline. My step paternal grandparents introduced me to the influence of wealth and how it may be used as a purposeful tool for the industry. My stepfather's sister filled my childhood triumphs with joy and laughter. A special uncle and aunt advised me on how to safely navigate the streets, and warned me about inevitable encounters with "gutter rat" people in the streets. My other aunts and uncles were character-shaping mentors who made a strong impact upon me as a young adult, and they were truly dear to my heart. There is one aunt who remains the open end part of my life, leaving me with no closure on account of her unexplained absence; I'm left with mixed emotions and incomplete feelings concerning her whereabouts.

I have a host of relatives who are no longer burdened with the trials and tribulations of this world, but will never be forgotten.

My lifeline: My mother equipped me with information that she felt would prepare me for whatever direction I chose to take in life. My father and stepfather showed me different impressions of what a father should be and could not be. My siblings all add color and texture to my life. My daughters—God's testimony of favor within my life, and God's gift to my life—have both kept me humble, tolerating me in spite of my mistakes. My nephew, what can I say? He's the son I never had.

The interruption in my bloodline: My granddaughters—my blessing, my everlasting joy, my hidden treasure. My minister—the man who showed me the power of spiritual love, support, and understanding through unspoken words. My foster children—God trusted me to nurture them to grow and become productive in society. My home-care provider, a.k.a. Auntie—my rock and my shield against the unexpected. And last but never not least, my right-hand girl—you know how to make me believe in me, in my vision, and in you.

Many thanks to all my relatives who allowed me to experience their direct and indirect presence through all the good and bad times in my life. The life shared with everyone connected to my bloodline enhanced and elevated me to a plateau high enough to realize I always have to look up to God.

ALISA D. BOYD

CONTENTS

Foreword ix

Acknowledgments xi

Introduction xiii

1   Looking Back at It 1

2   Filtering It 33

3   A State of Confusion about It 57

4   Beginning to Make Sense of It 63

5   Accepting Limitations of It 71

6   Speaking Victory over It 79

7   Deliverance from It 93

8   Bringing Closure to It 113

9   Equipped for War Because of It 119

10   Being Restored from It 133

Epilogue 141

Appendix – Praying through It 149

About the Author 157

FOREWORD

Alisa Boyd has done an arduous job of writing a book about her life. This "tell-all" book is a soul-searching account of what she had to endure, starting with her childhood and continuing through her life. Ms. Boyd's journey gives us a story of what could happen to anyone looking for the correct spiritual and moral direction, but only finding things that damage the soul. Ms. Boyd presents you, the reader, with insights culled from her life experiences. She offers you, the reader, a chance to interact with her by detailing your own experiences. We hope that this can help you make better decisions in your daily life. The book is powerful! It comes from the truths Ms. Boyd had to overcome before she was able to move forward with her life.

Ms. Boyd shows us that, with God's help, we can triumph over the unspeakable.

Dr. Melvin Sylvester
Long Island University

ALISA D. BOYD

ACKNOWLEDGEMENTS

I give honor to God for directing me to people who sincerely cared about helping me mature. The wise insights of people from all over the world have provided the foundation of this book.

I am thankful for the love and support of New Birth Missionary Baptist Church. I've found in them a nourishing place of worship that inspires my surrender, and praise of God.

A very special note of gratitude and appreciation is owed to Apostle Bishop Eddie L. Long and First Lady, Vanessa G. Long. I applaud the First Lady for her gentle criticism and keen direction the year I attended a Heart 2 Heart Conference in Savannah, GA. She taught me that my fear can limit the Spirit's effectiveness. She said, "We have to act; do something to confront the fear." The First Lady applied this scripture: "Jesus said unto him, If thou canst believe, all things *are* possible to him that believeth" (Mark 9:23 King James Version). Apostle Long sealed the deal during that same trip with encouraging words when he said, "Stop centering your attention on your hurt, and look at the vision the Holy Spirit gives you. The Holy Spirit cleared all the debts you thought you owed society." Those words gave me confidence and pushed me further to pursue my dreams.

Lots of love I give to my sister in Christ, Elder Bernice A. King. I am most grateful for her sermon entitled, "Deal with It." She spoke of how not dealing with "It" could turn into a stranglehold and become one's soul-tie with "It." She expressed that "It" can have you doing so bad that you will become a time bomb waiting to explode. She resonated with words on how to deal with "It-issues" and said, "You will not die with your dreams and destiny in you. You will live and declare the praises of God." I received that word, and now I'm able to walk in Victory.

My editor, Dr. Jackie S. Henderson, and co-writer my brother Nasrrudiyn Hakiym, you both have shown me true love in your effortless work to make this happen.

INTRODUCTION

My story is written to enlighten those whose life experiences have caused them to avoid dealing with resentment, shame, guilt, secrets, lies, anger, and betrayal. I hope this book acts as a compass that leads you to understand how faith can help you face your issues. I want everyone to understand how to unlock the emotional handcuffs that unwholesome living puts on our hearts. That freedom will allow your heart to embrace the idea of having a life full of hope, accomplishments, and purpose.

"Thine, O LORD, [is] the greatness; and the power, and the glory, and the victory, and the majesty: for all [that is] in the heaven and in the earth [is thine]; thine [is] the kingdom, O LORD and thou art exalted as head above all. Both riches and honor [come] of thee, and thou reignest over all; and in thine hand [is] power and might; and in thine hand [it is] to make great, and to give strength unto all" (1 Chron. 29:11-12 KJV).

When I was a child, love was expressed in a variety of confusing forms. Love was revealed in ways that ranged from brutalities to tender reconciliations. This language of love was as bewildering to me as a purple moon in a green sky. I rarely saw my parents displaying affection or sharing a warm embrace as a loving couple. They seemed more intimate when they were fighting and much colder when their fighting ended. Their example, coupled with the other perplexing experiences, seemed to suck the ability or desire to love right out of me and my sister. In the rare instances that healthy expressions of love came our way, they bounced off of us like raindrops.

My younger brother, on the other hand, had an intense reaction to our parents' behavior. He passionately loved everyone in the family. My two older brothers were able to emotionally divorce themselves from being devoted to my parents and, because they earned a little bit of money, were able to provide the rest of us with a small measure of the parental love we were lacking.

As I grew older, negative memories played like a never-ending movie in my head. During times of anguish, when something caught me off guard and snuck past my protective armor, there was nothing to stop the rush of tears. I would cry nearly every day, and the thought of "what might happen tomorrow" kept me constantly off balance.

I could not control my growing worries, but I was carefully hidden behind a smile. Foolish pride would not allow me to give voice to my uncertainties, and other than my grandparents, there were few people in whom I could confide.

By the time I was sixteen, I was enjoying the "glitz and glamour" of associating myself with drug dealers and other men with great wealth. The many dangers that accompanied welcomed (and unwelcomed) sex, as well as drugs and other resources used to get quick money, became quite real when I became a parent at the age of twenty-one.

I had this funny feeling that parents cursed their children with the things they do and say. By the time I turned twenty-five, I was raising three children, two daughters and a nephew as a son. I wanted to help my sister, but I needed help myself. However, during the most troublesome times in our lives, I realized we were not alone. I started going back to church and praying for my family. In spite of living with one of the most elusive drug dealers, the spirit of deliverance stood with us. For me, I recognized this one day while looking into the eyes of my children. I saw their innocence and how they needed me to protect them from many dangerous predicaments. Somewhere inside of me came the Scripture where God says, "He will never leave you nor forsake you." No, the skies did not open, and yes, there were still times when I wondered if the spirit of deliverance had left us. But I never forgot God's promise.

My first few years of being a single parent to three young children was a difficult road. I believed my children should have the best of everything, and I should get it for them by any means necessary. That's when I began to abandon my priorities as a parent. Yet, the most difficult part of parenting may have been raising my nephew as a son, and letting him call me mommy. My sister was very angry, but in my mind I wanted him to have a sense of belonging, since two of his four brothers were awarded to Montgomery County Children Services. I selfishly used him to fill the void of me not giving birth to a male child.

I wanted so much for my nephew, yet I learned what he really needed was a positive male role model. There were few men around for him to look up to, since most of the men in his life were corrupt to some degree. He would occasionally receive Godly influence from men in church. However, there were no men available to spend adequate time with. In fact, even I fell short, in terms of being able to spend the quality time with him that I felt he deserved.

Though he spent many years in counseling, no one stopped to hear his questions or understand why he sought so much attention. Many days he went to sleep wetting the bed and waking up to me spanking him with the closest thing I found. At that time I thought he was simply being lazy. Not once did I or anyone else consider that he had been robbed of hope and peace.

I tried my best, but after ten years, my best was not good enough to keep him away from the same judicial system that also found space for his other siblings. I learned from that experience that my nephew's problems needed more than just me. The pain of letting him go was indescribable.

A few years passed by, and one night, after falling asleep, something happened that was not a dream. I began feeling a wonderful sense of peace and tranquility. Then I began speaking to something inside of me.

I heard a voice say, "Everything is going to be all right. I'm going to make your name great."

And I said, "I don't take this opportunity for granted. I will serve You, Lord, with all my heart." I felt a new connection with someone different from the person I'd heard others talk about and the person I saw in the mirror.

I fell into a slumber, but was later awakened by a harsh voice saying, "You're crazy for listening to something speaking inside you."

The level of my insanity did not sit well in my mind. It was different from being crazy over a man, or going crazy at a championship game.

I tried to turn to the edge of the bed, but I could not move. I felt paralyzed. The enemy stood alongside me, redirecting my thoughts to seek help from my daughters, who were asleep in the bed next to me.

The sane part of my brain began wrestling with my ego, telling me to cry out, but I could not. I felt an unusual force silencing my voice. The force had gotten so strong, keeping me from moving, speaking, or crying. I thought I was dying.

That moment of distress caused me to call on the name of Jesus. The Holy Spirit instantly freed me from that unwanted spirit of captivity. With the help of the Spirit, I became aware of the supernatural power received from calling on the name of Jesus during my state of oppression.

The fact that most of my life has been lived in the shadow of unrighteousness has me cautious about the way I address situations. Yet along with my desire to avoid potential problems, inner strength closely follows fighting to keep in the forefront the practice of spiritual principles. Every day of my life is driven to trust The Most High God in my times of trouble. Though I may fall many times along my journey, I reach inside and stand up strong, smiling, with just one thought (and you can too)—"I Was Not Created To Break."

A little cookie to bite on

I learned that we must stop allowing the enemy to make us think the move we're making to change our life for the better is a mistake. No matter how impossible it looks, we have to trust and believe this is our set time by divine intervention. We can lift our voice and learn to give God praise for opening the window that leads to our purpose. Then use discernment to follow spiritually rooted directions to move in unfamiliar territory so we can help others as we gracefully walk into doors of opportunity.

I see why life can be like magnets. Like magnets, at some point it may be revealed that our unwholesomeness drew us to someone else's unwholesomeness. We fall for that person who is an imposter, sitting there taking up valuable time, hoping not to be found out. The cunning in that person causes us to lose our conscious state of mind, and we begin to see that person as a much-needed companion. However, it eventually comes out, and that's when relationships become toxic. Get out! Run for your life and don't look back.

I've seen many situations where no one likes to admit his own issues, but quickly blames others for theirs. What's worse is when relationships are established and both parties are pretending to love one another, while hiding their issues in an effort to keep from being exposed. Those relationships can end with mental breakdowns, or they can cause harm to your physical health. Own up to your own stuff and stop hiding from the truth.

The only person we can change is ourselves. If we deal with our issues and stop running from the things we fear, we can eventually establish healthier relationships. Remember, like magnets, healthy minds draw like minds. Yes, opposites do attract each other. That's when we have to recognize our assignment. Every attraction is not meant to be intimate. It may have been designed to help that person get through something, not to burden oneself with hurt or pain. Everything has a season. We have to pray for divine revelation to learn how to identify when the assignment is over.

Love is the greatest gift we can receive. If demonstrated improperly, one's whole world can be destroyed. Never love anyone more than God. Take a look in the mirror and repeat these words: "I love the Lord, I love myself, and I love others" --

It is our time to move on in God's world. We are **Not Created to Break!**

Chapter 1

LOOKING BACK AT IT

A wise man once said, "In life, there is a season for everything." After much contemplating and soul-searching, I found that this statement is a truism. So in acceptance of this fact, I came also to the understanding that this certainly must apply to me and my life as well.

The divine order of things makes it apparent that seasons change, and must change. Therefore, I had to take courage and see life as if it were a season. I said to myself, "I will not permit the chill of my life's experience of pain to freeze my soul, mind, and spirit into a state of no hope for healing, which comes in the summer of deliverance.

This principle was easier said than what it took to make it practical, but there is truly the season when my life sprang forward. Right now, allow me to share more of my life's journey toward understanding, acceptance, and deliverance. But for me to do so, I have to take you first through my season of hurt, disappointment, and pain.

As I look back upon my somewhat ornamented past, I see myself as a child living in California with my baby brother who was not even crawling, a little sister around two years old, and two older brothers. Mother and Daddy raised five children in a two-bedroom apartment, where they showed inappropriate punishments and a lack of nurturing.

Mother was adamant about children being seen and not heard. The closet was a place of punishment I shared with the oldest two boys, Andrew and Mike. It was very hard not to be mad when Mother sent me to the closet. After a while, the anger became numb and was transformed to mentally accepting the closet as a play room.

Instead of gravitating to abuse, it was more pleasant to focus on the impromptu entertainment seeing things outdoors from a peek window in the closet. Several old and crooked-over tenants roamed outside the two-story nursing home on the right side of our apartment. The window was high enough to also see the back yard of a gated luxury apartment complex. There was so much to admire behind that six-foot fence. The trees and grass were well maintained, and it secured a private area where two dogs caught Frisbees and ran after balls with their owner. Falling asleep in my special corner of the closet at night sometimes was more peaceful than sleeping in my bed.

My morning breakfast came with unwanted mealworms floating on spoonfuls of cereal. Taking that second trip to the kitchen usually meant it was the last meal for the day. The time of day did not matter; it was either lunch or dinner. Some days we had nothing on the stove but the sound of kernels popping and a lid rising. That sound summoned Mother's full attention to prepare our meal. I waited for the moment to savor the taste of salt and pepper on our popcorn. When Daddy got a job, we advanced to eating burgers from Jack in the Box and chicken from Jim Dandy.

The afternoon temperatures were mostly hot and very uncomfortable. By evening time I was usually sneaking into the bathroom, after being warned not to play in the water. I tried to figure out how to consume the drips of water streaming inside the rusted, dingy sink. That carefree adventure ended when Mother's brother visited us with his family. His wife's brother had a Doberman that was always so thirsty. My eyes lit up when seeing how satisfying it was for the dog to lick water from the toilet. (At five years old, I was still sipping water from the toilet to quench my thirst.)

I enjoyed watching Mother collect stamps in a booklet to get reward points for purchases on household items and other merchandise from a catalog. She saved enough booklets to purchase an outdoor metal swing and slide set. Playing outside and the attention we got from other children seemed great, but sometimes children were playing on our swings without us. With the help of the neighborhood children, we destroyed that swing set within months. The excitement of riding my big wheel, while racing my brothers on the sidewalk up and down the block was so fun.

Mostly everything Mother purchased for me, I shared with my sister, Jewel. Mother didn't buy us dolls; most of our toys were blocks, jump ropes, coloring books, and we had a huge electric train set that made noise. For me, playing with Jewel was the funniest time. Playing house was entertaining. I was the mommy, and Jewel was my baby. She followed me everywhere and did most things I told her to do. I loved making up games to play with her more than playing with the toys.

Then came along a heart-breaking experience. Mother, my little sister, who had been my best friend since I taught her how to talk, and my baby brother took a ride in an airplane back to Mother's hometown in Dayton, Ohio. Whatever news Mother got on the phone that day was enough for her to pack a few things and fly home.

Daddy did his best caring for the oldest three children. It wasn't so bad being with him. We got to run around and play more, and Daddy kept his word not to whup us, after being scolded by Mother's brother to keep his foot off our butts. He didn't whup me with his paddle when I cried while his buddy's wife was combing my hair and clothing me. It wasn't fun taking baths without Jewel. I even missed Mother's touch and the sound of her voice, even with her abusiveness.

We soon had to move out of our apartment, and Daddy gave a lot of our belongings away when we moved. Andrew, Mike, and I slept together on a couch, when Daddy moved us into a two-bedroom apartment with his cousin, who was married to a white lady. We were only allowed to go to the restroom, to the kitchen nook to eat, on the balcony with an adult, and in the living room, where we watched TV and slept.

What I really liked about being there was being able to eat lots of food and walk onto the balcony. It was nice standing on the balcony getting a bird's-eye view of the scenery displaying lots of lights, skyscrapers, bridges, and cars speeding so fast. The stars shining in the inky blue sky captured my eyes at night.

Even though we didn't get to play outside that often, it was fun getting out to play at the beach. Most days were spent watching cartoons and network shows with my two brothers until we fell asleep on their couch. We woke up most mornings smelling pancakes with bacon and eggs. Those scrumptious mornings ended on Thanksgiving Day, when we went from celebrating Thanksgiving with a big feast to eating turkey several days for breakfast, lunch, and dinner.

I had the biggest fear of the unexpected when Daddy said we were moving back to Dayton. It was time to get out from being cooped up inside that apartment; I just wasn't sure if we were moving to a worse or better place to live. Daddy had lots of talks with us about not wasting food, and making the best out of bad situations. The time we spent living in that apartment with that white lady and Daddy's cousin seemed like I had been separated three or four years from my sister and the touch of my chubby little brother's cheek. Could I have at least heard their voices?

The happiest day of my life was seeing Jewel again and receiving a warm hug from my baby brother, whom I always called Baby Brother. I couldn't control my tears. By no means was I sad. I tried to stop crying, but the excitement from seeing my family back together again made me cry. The anticipation from riding for days in the back seat of that Volkswagen Beetle was well worth the travel.

We stayed with Daddy's parents for a short time. Living in a house with our paternal grandparents was the best thing ever. Granddaddy built a three-bedroom brick house for his family. My grandparents slept upstairs with their young adult daughter, and even though there was an extra guest room, it was off limits for me and my siblings. The house had a living room, family room with office space, and a really big finished basement. Daddy entertained us with music and snacks from the wet bar and taught us how to play ping-pong in the recreation area. My siblings and I shared a pull-out couch, and we had a rollaway bed, while my parents slept in a room in the basement.

Granddaddy was rarely at home. He spent a lot of time working with his construction company, and when he wasn't working, he was fishing or hunting. He didn't allow us in the room designated for his office, and we were limited to playing in the backyard because he didn't want us disturbing the hunting dogs in the kennel. Most outdoor activities were spent on outings riding in Granddaddy's boat on the lake, taking trips to the park, and attending sports games with Daddy's sister.

Grandma was laid-back. I can't remember her having much interaction with us, but I always saw her cooking and cleaning.

Christmas was one of my favorite holidays. I enjoyed helping Daddy's sister decorate the tree with Grandma. The warmth of the chimney being lit was so comforting. I didn't have to wonder what my parents would get me for Christmas because Granddaddy told us to write a list of everything we wanted from Santa. I got every gift I wrote on my list. Aunty shopped at every kid's department store, toy store, K-mart, and wherever else she had to go to find the things on our list. She made sure Santa had everything wrapped and under the tree." We had our names on stockings filled with knick-knacks, bank envelopes filled with money, and an unforgettable Christmas feast with lots of sweets and nuts.

Mother and Daddy eventually moved us into a three-bedroom low-income apartment complex. Mother tried to meet our needs, but the beer, wine, and cigarettes had more control over her. There were days when I'd rather stay in my room than hear the chaos coming from her and Daddy.

I do not remember having birthday parties, but Daddy's family made sure we had gifts. Mother's sister, Aunt Liz, enjoyed having us at her children's birthday celebrations. Her daughter was a few years younger than I, and her son was my age. She took us swimming at the outdoor pool in their apartment complex, and we went to see shows at the neighborhood movie theater with them. I was happy when Mother's and Daddy's family members took us on outings. Those outings spent with our relatives gave me something to brag about.

On a bright, sunny day, I was with Andrew and Mike at the neighborhood pharmacy buying penny candy, and became very agitated when Andrew and Mike started talking to a strange man I had never seen before. They told me to come meet him. Fear overwhelmed me because we had always been warned not to talk to strangers. I told them we should go home before we got in trouble.

My brothers said, "This is our real father."

I was about to cry. I didn't know what that meant. I thought he was trying to steal us from our parents.

Andrew assured me that man was no stranger. He said Mother's older three children were by another man, and Daddy was only Jewel's and Baby Brother's real father. He remembered his face from pictures in Mother's photo album. I thought to myself, where has this man been all this time? Or better yet, why did he leave us?

There were so many questions in my little brain, but I was distracted from the pleasant scent of cologne and how attractive that man looked. He was well dressed and adamant about meeting me. He asked me my age and gave me money when I told him my birthday had passed a few days earlier.

I saw that man only once or twice after that day. Even though Mother confirmed he was my biological father, it did not register in my brain. After all I had been through as a child, life had not changed any, knowing who was my biological father.

Mother and Daddy were always drinking and fighting. Sometimes they would drink all day and pass out without feeding us. It sure would have been nice to be with my biological father during those times than to wonder why he couldn't spend time with me.

Andrew was our chef. He read recipes from the oatmeal box to make cookies and whipped up whatever else was edible. Spreading butter on bread and sprinkling it with sugar was my favorite. There was also times when we made our own candy by pouring sugar on a spoon and placing it on fire from the stove burner.

Our neighbors had great compassion for us. They had no problem feeding us when we asked for something to eat. One day, we walked across the parking lot to play with a little girl, and while writing with chalk on the sidewalk we stumbled on some edible grass, and boy was that good.

Living with my parents had gotten so bad, we used to plot to run away. One day we got halfway to Daddy's parent's house five miles away and turned around because we didn't want to leave Mother.

Daddy got the worse blows during their fights, but Mother got called some of the worst names. Mother did things to Daddy that had him in tears. She poured sugar in the tank of his truck, packed his clothes, and sometimes hid his work boots. Daddy even cried whenever he told us he was leaving her, but he always made his way back to her.

We lived in Dayton, Ohio for a few years before packing up and heading to Detroit, Michigan. Did they have a plan in mind?

Did it even matter that we would miss our friends? We spent a few days shacked up in the living room of some lady's house and had to call her Auntie, even though we knew she wasn't related to us. Her son accepted us as his fake cousins, so we all got along well.

We sat in the living room most nights telling spooky stories and saying the silliest mama jokes, while our parents danced in the kitchen nook and got drunk. Mother and Daddy seemed happy, as long as their hands were in close reach of a cup, and their fingers had a grip on a cigarette.

My siblings and I had gotten used to riding in the car with no clue where we'd end up. We sat many times for hours, sounding off the car alarm from opening the doors, while Mother and Daddy visited with friends.

One particular day, Daddy pulled up in a driveway two houses from Mother's sister's house and said, "This is our new home."

I could not believe my eyes. The grass in the front yard was so beautiful, and the backyard was fenced with a garage. Daddy opened the entry door, and we walked into a fully furnished house. I ran upstairs to see my bedroom. I shared a full-size bed with my sister, and we had a big closet. I ran downstairs through the living room to see the family room. It was my dream come true—a real home with very nice furniture.

Finally, my siblings and I were living in a beautiful house with my parents for the first time. This house had more than enough space for my siblings and me, my parents, and family members who wanted to spend the night. We had an all-white living room with white furniture and accessories. The dining room furniture had a matching china cabinet. The playroom was spacious, with a brown sectional sofa and a large color TV, and the basement was not finished, but nice enough to play hide-and-seek and other games.

The neighborhood children were very nice, and it was important to me to meet new friends. I played a lot of hand games, hopscotch, and learned double-dutch jump rope. I took advantage of the opportunity and the quality time I got to spend with my cousins who lived two houses away. I'd run to their house whenever Mother and Daddy started arguing and fighting.

Weekends and summer vacation were spent with Mother's parents. There was no place like my maternal grandparents' home in Detroit, Michigan, where they had a beautifully landscaped two-story house on Murray Hill Street with a big backyard that was well maintained for Mother Dear's beautiful garden, and a detached garage.

The house had two bedrooms upstairs, with two attics. One of the attics was adjoining a bedroom, while the other attic was near the stairway. The master bedroom was on the first floor, and there was a beautiful piano sitting in the living room just a few feet away. The basement was very spacious with a room under the stairwell that was used as an office.

That house had more than enough space to hide the unspeakable deeds that my loving grandparents would never have believed could happen under their roof.

*

Rev was a minister in the local church. Everyone called him Rev. His wife was fondly called Mother Dear. They gave birth to eleven children, nine of whom lived in Michigan, a daughter lived in Ohio, and the other daughter lived in Alaska. Only five of their children lived with them, yet he maintained a close-knit family. Everyone he met got an invitation to get saved and receive the blessings of the Lord.

Two of Mother's brothers and one sister lived within walking distance from each other. We were geographically located two houses from Aunt Dee Dee, a few blocks from Uncle Ron, a few miles from Uncle Frank, and farther down a few more miles was my grandparent's house.

The times I traveled from house to house, I observed Aunt Dee Dee and a few of the male's girlfriends dressing up in fancy clothes, quite different from the clothes I saw women wear to church. The men in the family seem to give their approval with their girlfriends' sluttish outfits. But whenever they were around Mother Dear, she would whip out safety pins to close up their garments.

There was lots of excitement in our family. Along with the many dog fights, there was gang activity, and a humongous distribution of drugs. It was no secret that some of the male relatives were in the pimp game. Women getting beat were a common thing for me to see. Under my umbrella of life were live actions portrayed in movies like *Sparkle*, *Car Wash*, *Lady Sings the Blues*, and *The Godfather*.

The younger children were left home alone most of the time, after being exposed to situations and experiences never intended for a child. Nevertheless the children always looked forward to spending weekends and school vacations at the house of Rev and Mother Dear.

The behaviors of pimps and prostitutes were exemplified by most of the adults in the family: men and women wearing furs, expensive clothes, and females in lingerie with high heels. This shaped the role play of the children most of the time when playing house.

It was fun seeing Baby Brother dressed up in little girl's clothes when we played house. Being skinny usually left me unpicked as a counterpart paired up as boyfriend and girlfriend.

So I was contented with playing board games, tic-tac-toe, or SOS on the chalkboard in the basement. I did this with my little sister and younger cousins. We also had the most fun taking turns sharing our only pair of skates in the basement.

Rev seemed determine to save souls, and that's how he ran his house, exalting Christ and equipping us as believers. Mother Dear taught us Bible stories and prayed with us, while Rev studied the Word in his office, located near a short entryway, under the stairs in the basement. He always kept the door locked to his study room.

One day while everyone was playing upstairs, I stumbled upon a skeleton key in the kitchen. Determination was in me, after repeated attempts of trying to push the key to open the door to Rev's office. I jiggled it around in the keyhole one last time, and it opened the door. I slowly pushed the door open to see what was in his study room. I had a creepy feeling as I flipped the light switch on. The dimmed light revealed my shadow, and yet it felt as if I were not alone.

From a glance, it seems as if the room had a million books stacked on a dark wooden bookshelf layered with dust. On the opposite side of the wall, there was a huge metal cross. On one side of his desk a bottle of oil stood next to a large Bible, with a red cloth ribbon hanging as its bookmark.

The scenery on the wall across from his desk was a somber portrait symbolizing Jesus having dinner with his disciples. Rev's office was dark and felt cold. I think the eyes in the picture made me nervous. I had the eerie feeling that Jesus' eyes stared at me everywhere I walked. I rushed out of there having no intentions of returning.

I didn't know what to expect when staying at my grandparents' house. Some of my best times were spent with my relatives, and there was never a dull moment. My heart was filled with excitement when my ruthless male cousin brought his neighbor over to play house. I finally had a boyfriend. My cousin urged me to follow them down the hall and into my aunt's bedroom. I was easily lured into the attic adjoining the bedroom. We often ducked and hid in that attic when playing hide-and-seek.

I never anticipated my cousin would cross the line with me. The lights went off, and then I found myself struggling to hold down and onto my skirt. I tried to yell for help, but one of them muffled my mouth. Soon afterwards my panties were ripped, and I went crazy biting, scratching, kicking, and punching all at the same time. My cousin thought it was some kind of joke, even though he unsuccessfully tried to make me have sex with his neighbor. Neither of them was in their teens, so the severity of the situation and me being eight years old was the farthest thing from their mind.

All the children ranging from toddlers to teenagers had been exposed to events and things unappealing to religious persuasion. It appeared that none of the adults had any idea or even had any consideration about what took place in Rev's house. They trusted that we all were in good care with our grandparents.

But that was the real problem. There were ten to fifteen children left home alone. We were not in good care. I was in the midst of a sexually imposed dilemma, while Rev and Mother Dear seemed to have failed us all with teaching the ways of the Lord. I adored my grandparents, yet at the same time, I knew some things we were doing in their home were not right.

As I think back I see why Mother Dear always kept her family in prayer, and I also understand why she often quoted this passage from Joshua 1:9 (NKJV). "Have not I commanded thee? Be strong and of a good courage; be not afraid, neither be thou dismayed: for the LORD thy God *is* with thee whithersoever thou goest."

I saw myself, that confused little nine-year-old girl, nursing a strange feeling that Mother and Daddy was about to be held accountable for all the awful things that had happened in their house on the 15000 block of Lauder Street.

My six-year-old baby sister Jewel, while being unsupervised, was molested by a teenager in our garage. Finding Jewel on her knees with a guy standing over her had me distraught.

All I could think to say was, "Ooh, Jewel, you better stop that. You gonna get in big trouble!"

She yelled back, "Don't tell. You can have this sucker."

I was so hurt to see my sister being treated that way. I ran in the house yelling to Mother, "Some boy got Jewel in the garage doing something nasty."

That guy was badly beaten by my relatives, and no one ever spoke a word about what happened after that day.

A few months later, my parents' lack of attention coupled with Jewel's childlike imagination had our whole family facing the old saying of curiosity kills the cat. You see, Uncle Spoon, wasn't doing well at home with his parents, so Mother invited him to move in with us. He was taking medicine daily for his paranoid schizophrenia personality disorder. Somehow, Jewel stumbled upon Uncle Spoon's colorful psych meds. I caught her eating one of the pills, and she tried convincing me that it was a jellybean. I knew better, so I forced her to spit it out.

Hours later, I and my other siblings trembled as Mother blamed and cussed us out because Jewel had begun running up the stairs, banging walls, and having loud conversations with herself as a result of toxic poisoning. She was rushed to the hospital and stayed there a few days to get the medicine flushed out of her system.

On other occasions, Mother didn't intervene in domestic abuses inflicted by her brothers upon their girlfriends. This often occurred in our kitchen, living room, bathroom, and basement. In another instance, Daddy was too crippled by alcoholism to stand firm enough to substantially manage the house properly. He used violence against Mother to get his point across, which was usually the way he demonstrated being the man of the house.

The strange feeling inside me became manifest when two men rang the doorbell and forced their way into our house, waving guns, badges of authority. Everything seemed to happen so fast after they handed Daddy the legal papers. The men immediately began throwing out our furniture and personal belongings. Since we didn't have the luxury of luggage, we used garbage bags to pack our belongings, with the majority of our things stuffed into blankets and large sheets.

Andrew and Mike, my elder brothers, had a difficult time keeping our dogs from attacking those men. My eldest brother, Andrew, gave our German Shepherd informal training to protect the family, but our Doberman had been trained in obedience school to attack at the sight of a gun. The men warned Daddy to secure the dogs, or they were going to shoot them. My brothers locked the dogs in the garage until we were able to transport them to Mother's oldest brother, Uncle Craig's house.

The house had previously belonged to my grandparents, before they moved back to Ohio so Rev could start his own church. Uncle Frank, who always held the deed, rented the house to his brother Craig. Moving in with Uncle Craig was one of the most degrading, humiliating, and horrific experiences for me.

Uncle Craig was in his forties and had a younger girlfriend named Shari in her twenties. Shari came into their relationship with her three-year-old daughter Tonya. Later between them, they had a daughter Nicole, who was diagnosed with Down syndrome.

Babysitting Uncle Craig's daughter Nicole gave me motivation. Nicole had a look on her face I'd never seen before, but that Mongoloid look became so lovable to me. I sat in the room with Shari whenever the nurse came to observe the progress with Nicole's motor skills. I cried when I saw Uncle Craig's eyes fill with tears as he sat in a corner turning up a liquor bottle and crying out of control. He had just received news from Shari that, according to the doctor, Nicole's lifespan may be short. I sang songs to Nicole and reminded her that she was beautiful. I needed her to live. My life would have been empty without her.

Seeing Nicole beat all the odds against her made me happy. Yet my sadness was something that shadowed me. It often came over me when I got Nicole from Uncle Craig's bedroom. This was especially hard on the times when I had to go back to get her a change of clothes or Pampers.

Once I stumbled upon Uncle Craig and Shari performing sexual acts with other people. Additionally, I was extremely disturbed when I saw Uncle Craig snapping pornographic pictures of Shari with these different men. That sick environment was accompanied with a dresser full of marijuana, assorted pills, and packets filled with cocaine.

The spiritual atmosphere of what was left of the house in the wake of my grandparents' move to Ohio was no longer there. When my grandparents were there, I remember the religious songs being sung, the piano being played, and prayers being said throughout the day and night.

That memory gave way to a new reality. Spiritual songs became rhythm and blues. Where there was the playing of piano, there now was playing of schemes. And the consistency of prayer had been replaced with the desire for the hustle.

Trust issues were my constant companion. It was hard for me to feel safe and trusting after being ripped from the freedom and security of the first place I called a home while living in Detroit. It appeared as if I was to grow up with a spiritual diet of torment, physical and mental pain, and the added effects of substance abuse. There was always on my plate of life a feeling of insecurity, hopelessness, and fear.

Even the breadwinner of the family had unspeakable secrets minded by abuse. The shock of being asked to clean blood from the bathroom walls caused me to pee on myself. This blood was due to a severe beating endured by Mimi. Uncle Frank had beaten his girlfriend so bad, her arm was broken, her lip was busted, her eyes were black, and she had bruises all over her body. And he still forced her to help me clean the blood off the floors and walls. After that day, I no longer begged to go places with the uncle I'd once idolized. Seeing that other side of him made me so afraid of what he might do to me if I made him mad.

As I looked back, I have terrible memories of fights. I often saw blood draining at the death of someone's dog during my relatives' many dog fights. I also saw the bruised flesh and broken bones of most of my male relatives' girlfriends as a result of their fights.

I wished things could have been different in that house on Lauder Street. After coming from the projects, it appeared that I was then growing up in an upscale neighborhood. Living in that neighborhood gave me comfort and a delightful feeling. What helped me to overcome unhappy feelings was the feel of freedom and security at the first place I could call home. It was there where I was able to create my own sense of peace and joy by spending quiet times alone.

My strength somehow was in my afflictions. I felt like a princess in my own wonderland. I sat in a corner beside the couch in the living room and sometimes beside the china cabinet in the formal dining room with thoughts of being in a castle. Sitting alone in those quiet places were very enjoyable to me. I would fantasize about a knight in shining armor coming to rescue me.

Whenever my siblings came looking for me, I'd run into the den and get prepared for family time. That was a time for me to play board games, eat popcorn, and watch network television with the family. We were all happy during those times.

However, those wonderful days usually came to an end with nights interrupted by drunken voices and grown folks arguing and fighting in our house. No lullabies were softly whispered as I drifted off to sleep. I escaped into slumber from the sounds of raging voices echoing through my bedroom vents. When I drifted off to sleep, I saw my knight in shining armor coming to rescue me on a white horse.

I understood pain enough to be able to relax in other uncomfortable places. You see, while living with Uncle Craig and his family, most bedroom stories and youthful activities started out well. As adolescents, we engaged in many time-consuming games, such as hide-and-seek and "Simon Says." But as time passed by and puberty rushed in, the games mysteriously became twisted into "Hide and Go Get 'Em," "Spin the Bottle," "In the Dark," and "Don't You Tell." Cousins would often stop by to visit us, adding their own versions to games being played, and my family's circumstances.

It did not seem long before evil came and cast shadows of despair and resentment upon what was already becoming our shady lives. Mother agreed to sign a lease to rent living space for us in the basement. How could she do that? I slept on the floor, sharing a mattress with my younger sister and brother, while my older brothers slept on the couch. There was no TV or any children activities to entertain us in the basement, so we spent a lot of time outside.

I was always fearful of Mother, yet it was a respectful fear with a foundation of understanding. That understanding was the devastating potential of her oncoming wrath. She became violent whenever and if ever some nonsense crossed her path. Mother, Daddy, the kids, and our pets living in a basement was truly nonsense, I thought.

Yet the idea of Uncle Craig and Shari to use the upper level as an after-hour bootleg joint making dollars made a little sense, I reasoned. They sold single cigarettes, alcoholic beverages, and to add a little spice, sometimes Shari sold dinners.

Then there was minute-by-minute renting of bed space for the selling of sex, drug deals, drug use, and exchange of stolen property. Things got out of hand a lot of times, but the unusual events that took place upstairs were not as despairing as what I had experienced during my existence in the basement.

Mother and Daddy seemed to be contented with sleeping in the basement, while taking orders from Shari to cook and eat at designated times. Burners were removed from the stove, and locks were fastened on the doors and cabinets in the kitchen, just in case someone chose to disobey the rules. This was a constant reminder to my primary family that we were restricted to living in the basement. Thinking back, I barely can remember taking hot baths or washing up properly.

It seemed as though my rooted resentment toward my parents had later branched out to become bitter fruits of motivation. I stayed outdoors most of the time to avoid hearing the adults arguing. A lady who lived a few houses from us saw me braiding Nicole's hair and asked if she could pay me to braid her two little girls' hair. I got permission from Mother to go up the street, but I didn't tell her the lady was paying me to do their hair. Having my own money helped me get myself and my little sister and brother stuff from the neighborhood store and the ice-cream truck.

I stayed at the house up the street almost every day from sunup until sundown. Those children seemed to be raising themselves. We were given hush-money whenever we stumbled on their mom engaging in some of the same sexual perversions I saw with my uncle and his girlfriend.

It was our dogs, Bullet and Princess, who brought some excitement into my life. It was fun running and being chased by them, as well as teaching them new tricks. This was my way of escaping the neglect and injustice I received in a place that was supposed to provide me security.

I loved that feeling of affection rubbing them and seeing their faces filled with excitement and joy when it was time to feed them. I was also intrigued when I saw their puppies; one or two died, and the others provided our family with extra income.

At times when I felt I had no one to talk to about the awful things going on around me, I was able to embrace the dogs, allowing me to overcome the feelings of anger and bitterness. I hadn't overcome my pain, but I felt good applying myself in a positive way to bring happiness to the dogs.

"For so is the will of God, that with well doing ye may put to silence the ignorance of foolish men: As free, and not using

[your] liberty for a cloak of maliciousness, but as the servants of God" (1 Peter 2:15-16 KJV).

Daddy tried hard to provide for our family, working at part-time jobs, and making sure we had food to eat. But it seemed like his alcoholic lifestyle took up residence with his personal issues, and neither seemed to give much credence to the expression of gentle paternal affections. When he got upset with Mother, he treated her like a stranger on the streets.

Mother did her best to fill any living space we occupied with some semblance of structure. She prepared meals and made sure all her children were together when it came time for rest. But it appeared as though her defects of character were too abrasive and bitter to allow any truthful measure of home sweet home. She closed her heart and mind to the abuse that happened right under her nose.

I would escape into lessons in school dreading every awful experience or dynamic of life spent in Mother's and Daddy's world. I was a little girl using my perception of their world as fuel for motivation. I visualized having a spirit to destroy any idea or cycle that would permit such things ever to be repeated in my life.

Once again, we packed up and headed back to Dayton, Ohio. By this time, I was used to being shifted from pillar to post. That day while sitting and looking out the window, I saw this little bird that appeared to be happily singing its heart out. I could feel in my heart that it was singing just to me. It seemed to really care about me. It knew I needed so much. But most of all, it knew I needed someone to know that I even existed.

This songbird knew I was hurting and alone, and needed some comfort. Comfort from its song.

I'm not sure what that bird saw in me, but I felt he was led there to inspire and encourage me after I learned the Bible verse in Matthew 6:26 (KJV) which says, "Behold the fowls in the air; for they sow not, neither do they reap, nor gather into barns; yet your heavenly Father feedeth them. Are ye not much better than they?"

I began to look ahead and always appreciated hearing chirps from birds. It's like music to my ears. I am not a songwriter, but I put together words inspired by that bird which helped me to deal with my environment and my unsettled condition.

A POWERLESS CHILD RECEIVES RESTORATION

FROM A SONG

Who was there to PROTECT her?
She often saw a songbird singing
Is what she supposed.
When "It" stared at her, the window was closed.
Mom and Dad were dazed by their drinking.
She gazed at her brothers and sister wondering,
How are they sleeping?
She rarely saw the darkness of night come to an end.
The light is dim, if there is a day - where has it been?

Who was there to SAVE her?
She's a child with no concern, and no means to be.
The closet was her place of discipline.
Often scolded for being a kid,
She joked and played to keep from crying.
She could only wonder why people were so deceiving.
Many times she thought, if I hid, would anybody see me?

Who was there to NURTURE her?
She waited for a Knight in Shining Armor.
All she saw was the horse lady coming from a mythical open field.
The imp in her life appeared like a full-course meal
Her cup ran over from long-winded fuss,
Drunken moments dried out from broken parental promises.
Sugar on a spoon over the stove burner was a treat to savor.

Who was there to COMFORT her?
Unpaid bills purchased unwanted breath-cold
and full of distress
She put on a coat and lay between the mattresses.
The powers to vacate came—and they drew guns.
Out went the furniture and out went the clothes.
She waddled around like a helpless hog.
Glad that they didn't kill her dogs

Who was there to SHELTER her?
Living in a basement was affordable, she supposed.
There were limitations to amenities when she arose.
Potential knowledge of these conditions at school
became a constant fear:
People smelled her unwashed clothes,
after her long jog there.
The sound of laughter was nothing nice.
Jokes received by children, black and white.
They teased her and called her poor.
Mom and Dad drank and smoked every day.
They had a little money, she would say.
Un-sobered eyes watch over her
while incest posed a test

Who was there to BEFRIEND her?
The closeness felt toward her brothers and sister
was like the sting of a bee.
They slept cramped together like little sardines.
She often wondered if her sister felt the same caress.
Time passed by with her secret promise kept.
The joy of summer was a blast.

In an inner city swim-mobile she played,
while wearing a dress.
Her dress was not even suitable
for a fire-hydrant splash.

Who was there to WELCOME her
with the feeling as if she belonged?
Mostly failed attempts to make friends
in the neighborhood,
because their parents didn't want her there.
She loved when her dog had puppies.
She played with them because she knew they cared.
Her friend imaginary came into sight doing everything he could.
In her he found no wrong that made her feel real good.

Who was there to UPHOLD her?
She lived in darkness for so very long.
In general conversations, anyone could see
She was a child searching for affection
from Mommy or Daddy.
Her friend imaginary told her to trust and believe in Him.
He opened an un-imaginary window so she could hear
The songbird singing in the crisp clean air.

Somewhere in life, we all may have been abused, or an abuser. When was the last time you questioned if you were going to ever obtain peace or serenity because of things that wronged you or the things you did wrong? Can you allow the peace of honesty to uplift you in an effort to own up to your own participation without blaming others? Allow the spirit of truth to empower you during your praiseworthy state of progress.

_____

_____

_____

_____

_____

_____

_____

"Nay, in all these things we are more than conquerors through him that loved us. For I am persuaded, that neither death, nor life, nor angels, nor principalities, nor powers, nor things present, nor things to come, Nor height, nor depth, nor any other creature, shall be able to separate us from the love of God, which is in Christ Jesus our Lord" (Romans 8:37-39 NIV).

Chapter 2

FILTERING IT

Wherever I looked, there always seemed to be something going on. Arguments between my parents, disagreements with relatives, altercations with classmates, and sibling rivalry were the least of things I faced. And as things would always have it, at one point or another, it would always come back to hurt me. Mother seemed to have a death ear, while Daddy was more concerned about giving me business lectures, but neither cared to listen to my problems. I was always looking around, wondering when the next tragedy would fall. I realize that this is a bad way to live. But that was how I lived my life.

There was so much negativity and pain. I often wondered, Why was I born? Why was I chosen to go through life this way? What good would come to anybody who has to struggle daily this way?

I had a difficult time trying to enjoy life. Holding on to bad memories created unwelcome pain. A childhood trauma resurfaced and struck me so badly, I eventually confronted life having stifled emotions. Insecurity and distrust toward others were unsocial emotions that emerged from the disgust of my trauma. I didn't know how to properly express my desire for love. In addition, feelings of being rejected by my biological father and unloved by my mother sent me running to the synthetic comfort of the streets.

The upbringing imparted from my parents left me with inadequate tools to build inner stability in the aftermath of emotional dilemmas, leading to my meltdowns. The greater friction of troubles in my life was a direct result of me allowing my focus to be centered on being raised in an unstable home. Then, I did not understand the role of a mother and a father. I saw the physical appearance of parents, but alcoholism made it impossible for them to administer, or for me to receive, efficient parenting. I longed to have someone provide me with a rich enough experience of love and kindness to offset the limited nurturing that left me feeling empty and defiled.

My older brothers hustled the streets and took penitentiary chances to provide me with material things that most girls could only dream of. When I turned eighteen, I chose to adapt my life to their shady practices of the streets. My appetite for a salvation experience left me. I became ego-driven and intoxicated by glossy celebrations.

Emotional disturbances followed me everywhere. When I looked into the mirror, I no longer saw the child of God my grandparents raised me to be. I saw a teenager, wounded and full of afflictions. My newly altered sense of morality justified negative behavior and, in turn, ignited my tongue with a voice inflamed with profanity.

Putting unappealing experiences upon shelves was my specialty during the early stages of my bondage. But The Most High's law of gravity later brought what I put up to the must-come-down reality of fearless confrontation. Life wasn't all bad, nor was it all pleasant, but nevertheless, there I was holding on to what my grandparents taught me. The Spirit saw me through as long as I committed to believing I could, would, and should overcome my battles. I wanted to believe I was created for the Kingdom. Yet, the sinful nature I developed added guilt as well as more pain to my feelings of distress. These feelings truly left me in a state of confusion.

The only thing I could hold on to was words from the following scripture: "When thou passest through the waters, I *will be* with thee; and through the rivers, they shall not overflow thee: when thou walkest through the fire, thou shalt not be burned; neither shall the flame kindle upon thee" (Isaiah 43:2 KJV).

One day I was quietly contemplating on what was going to happen next. I watched my fourteen-year-old sister struggle to care for her son, and I could not be of any assistance to her. I was searching to find my own way through life. Lessons learned in the streets were something more than I ever thought I could survive, while trying to find myself at eighteen years old.

I went from graduating high school to running away to a life corrupted by illegal drug activities and prostitution. Later I found myself moving in with a man of a different race. Living in a fairy tale was all I could make of his broken commitments and betrayal. I walked away from owning a new Jaguar, but more importantly, I refused to live with a man who was losing his inheritance to a freebasing habit (smoking cocaine in a pipe).

It was easy for me to hook up with a "drug dealer" on the rebound. Riding around in a fancy car and wearing expensive clothes was the norm for me now. By the time I turned nineteen, my life had been threatened with a gun by two different men I was dating. Those incidents made me understand why my brother Mike was so protective of me with respect to dating.

Where were we when our little sister needed us? She was no longer my baby sister, but life circumstance canceled every opportunity for her to mature into becoming anything more than my little sister.

My thoughts took me to those fun times, the days I nurtured her as if she were my baby, and being best friends for so long. I wish I could have been there to give her a shoulder to lean on, but

I thought my life was way too complicated to help anyone. I was too busy playing mind games with men, trying to be the center of attraction.

Doors of opportunity opened for me, and my life seemed to be headed in a better direction when Uncle Frank came home from doing time in the penitentiary. My brother Andrew asked if I would consider moving to Detroit to help maintain the family businesses. Uncle Frank was investing his drug money into rehabbing houses, duplexes, and apartment units. He also made every attempt to expand his pest control company.

As good as things seemed, it wasn't easy leaving my sister, who was dodging school and struggling to care for her newborn baby, and saying farewell to my baby brother. I packed up to move to what I believed to be a more promising life in Detroit, assisting my cousin with managing the family-owned pest control company.

My first year in Detroit I encountered some of my greatest tragedies. I became part of a drug cartel operated under the influence of Uncle Frank. We were having daily meetings on how to speak in Morse code, how to handle drug transactions, and how to identify undercover police officers. Seeing junkies from all walks of life (lawyers, accountants, business owners, and realtors) surprised me. My family was known for rescuing other families from losing their homes, helping restore their utilities, and providing weekly supplies of food, due to clients' excessive drug use. It was devastating seeing people die from overdoses of drugs.

My cousin and I were responsible for the upkeep of the main house. We secured enormous stacks of money and food stamp books, as well as priceless gemstones. Assortments of drugs were distributed like food delivered from a carry-out restaurant.

I'm not even sure what was worse, the IRS confiscating things or houses being raided. I was so upset when the doors were kicked in at the main house during one of the ATF raids. Someone called and alerted us to clean house. We expected the police to terrorize everyone and take undocumented jewelry and money. The hardest thing for me that day was trying to understand why the police took my high school yearbook as evidence. My yearbook was filled with photos from the fun memories before and during high school. Yet that could never be as devastating as having the feds confiscate my uncle's Rolls-Royce.

I had my share of celebrations with the family and outside entertainment: partying in the VIP rooms in most clubs, having front row seats at most main events, and attending celebrations with celebrity clients. On any given day, I was seen riding in a

Mitsubishi Sapporo, Jaguar, stretch Rolls-Royce, two-door Mercedes, Cadillac, Corvette, or Honda. My best times were spent during house parties with close associates and relatives.

I'd dated a few guys but never had a lasting relationship. The life I had begun to adapt to was not pleasing to me. I wanted to get control of my life and get my priorities back on track. I got a job working as a secretary for the head nurse at Sinai Hospital. That didn't last long, once I found out I was pregnant. My unexpected pregnancy upset me at first, until I saw the ultrasound of my baby. Seeing that picture gave me hope of having someone I could love and who could love me in return. Establishing a relationship with the father was not important to me.

I went through a lot of emotional issues while carrying my baby, which I almost miscarried. That didn't stop me from arguing and wanting to fight over any little thing.

Just when I thought I had my situation under control, I learned my little sister was knocked up with her second child a few months behind me. That had me so concerned. I didn't get to talk to her that often once she moved in with her boyfriend. The only time we communicated was when I went to Dayton on special occasions to visit everyone.

I looked forward to taking a trip to see my immediate family before I had my baby. I expected that trip to take away some of my distress from worrying about my family.

I planned my trip to Dayton with one of my cousins, whom I had just met a year before I moved to Detroit. She went on a date with my boyfriend's buddy when she came for a short visit. They were looking forward to seeing each other again. She convinced my boyfriend and his buddy to come to Dayton once I got there. We planned a candle-lit dinner the first night, and the next morning we had a big breakfast. The joy of that trip ended during our visit to the Salem Mall. I saw security escorting my pregnant little sister, who had just got done fighting outside of one of the stores in the mall.

When I got home, there were many questions in my head about the safety of my little sister. Is she ready for another baby? Will that guy be a good father for her baby? Will either of us know how to be a mother? I wanted what was best for my sister as well as for me. I found myself dealing with the same dramatic spirit I saw in my sister. Neither of us considered the harm we could cause to our babies.

I thought I would be more contented working with my cousin to keep Uncle Ken's pest control company open when he relocated his family to Dayton, Ohio. However, the anger in me grew much stronger. Both of our lives were full of so much negativity. All I could think of was, What's next?

Some words clearly came to me—*"Don't ever think that you know everything. You are NOT God."* Those were the words that stuck with me and one day caused me to stop in my tracks while thinking negatively. I was able to take the time and really think beyond myself. I realize even the smallest thing had meaning and a purpose. As that purpose is fulfilled, the results are unthinkable and may affect many people.

I wrote a short story about a simple, everyday can. It came to me as a narrative from my lifestyle as a young adult. This story helped me release things from my wounded little heart.

This story about the can is written from my experience as a wounded child. The many tribulations in my life and toxic thinking led me to believe I didn't have what it takes to tell my story. But I had to learn to filter out negative things in my life.

*

"The Can"

Before opening the doors of the neighborhood grocery store, the manager made an early morning inspection. He noticed an odd size can sitting on the wrong shelf. *How in the world did that can get over there?* he pondered. *That young man has got to do better when stocking these shelves.*

The first shift stockperson was offended when the manager accused him of making that mistake. He took pride in his work. He arrived to work early every day, signed for merchandise if the manager was not available, and also made sure sale items were stored properly for customers' easy access. Watching him stock the shelves often intrigued the store manager.

"I didn't leave that can there," the stockperson said.

The manager asked, "Well, how did it get there?"

"I don't know. Maybe you should ask someone from second shift. I always keep the shelves in order, in case you didn't know that."

"Don't deride me. Put the can where it belongs and make sure that mistake doesn't happen again."

"Are you serious, man? I really wish that can could talk and tell us both how it got there."

"Whatever!"

In an effort to abate the manager's discontentment, the stockperson tried to humor him. Yet, little did he know the manager was already in a grumpy mood before he came to open the store. The stockperson's ego was crushed, and he clearly did not mind showing it. The rolling of his eyes reflected how he felt inside, as he walked toward the other side of the store.

The manager shook his head as he fumbled in his pocket for keys to unlock the doors. He also made a mental note of the rudeness displayed by the stockperson.

It was no secret among the employees about the manager's harshness toward them, yet the irrational treatment displayed troubled the stockperson. Nevertheless, the stockperson chose to regroup and got past the morning's disruption. Diligently performing his duties as stock clerk, his strong dedication to his job, and his humble acceptance of the manager's treatment earned him the privilege of remaining on first shift.

Tolerating mistreatment from the manager was an unspoken given. The manager somehow believed the stockperson owed it to him due to the promise of becoming assistant manager, after receiving his associate degree within six months.

A beautiful young lady fascinated the stockperson as she strolled toward him in the middle of the aisle. "Excuse me, do you work here?" she asked.

"Yes. How may I help you?"

"I'm looking for the honey roasted peanuts on sale."

"Follow me. I'll show you the aisle where they're stocked," he replied. As the stockperson led the lady to her destination, he tossed the unusual can into a miscellaneous cart catty-cornered on the other side of the aisle.

The stockperson was busy all afternoon scanning merchandise and replenishing heavy items on their shelves. By the end of his shift, he noticed the can in the miscellaneous cart with some of the soon-to-be-expired items. While he pushed the cart near the stockroom door, he thought to himself, *Another clerk can transfer this can to the basket with the other marked-down items.*

A second shift clerk arrived a few minutes late. He rushed to arrange the shelves with items from the miscellaneous basket. He clumsily fumbled with the marked-down items from the basket, causing the unusually sized can to slip from his grip and roll under a display sign. Hastily, he tried to retrieve the can, but it had rolled too far for his hand to reach.

Later that evening, the cleaning crew entered the building and immediately started sweeping. One member swept the can from under the display sign, and it quietly rolled to the center of the store along with other trash.

Another member put the pile of trash into a huge Glad garbage bag and huffed and puffed as he tossed it into a dumpster. He heard a sound similar to the meow of a cat. There it was again and again. Louder! He looked into the dumpster and saw that it was a baby.

The authorities were notified, and the news channel quickly got their top story for the evening. Who could do such a thing? There was lots of hope and prayers in the community that both the mother and the baby were safe.

The mother showed up at the hospital the next day suffering from bipolar schizophrenia disorder. She had gone days without taking her medicine and flipped out. The baby was placed in the custody of Family and Children Services.

The oversized can remained in the belly of the dumpster for several days because of the holiday. The city's central compactor was jammed from being overloaded with garbage, which delayed sanitation workers from completing their routes on time.

Upon the sanitation workers' arrival to the grocery store's dumpster, they haphazardly performed their jobs. Several bags ripped opened, and trash flew everywhere. The can rolled down the alley, abruptly stopping by the curb at the corner.

Later that day, there was a terrible storm and strong winds forced the can to roll from the curb down a hill along the streets. Rain continued to fall for several days. The can eventually found its way into a ditch.

A few adolescent boys splashing their way through puddles spotted the can. One of the boys kicked it across the street, and then they all took turns kicking the can down the block. In their minds, they were playing a championship game of inner city soccer. They soon lost interest as they discussed games to be played on the chubby boy's PlayStation 2, and quickly raced to his house to embark upon the game "Call of Duty."

The next day a group of high school students saw the can by a tree. It was dented up and the label torn off. They pitched it toward one another and took turns batting it with a stick. One of the boys hit the can so hard, it flew over a fence.

They kept it moving when they saw the "Beware of Dog!" sign.

A scraggly-looking dog dug up dirt to bury the can, but it didn't do an adequate job.

Not long afterwards, blowing winds uncovered the can. Darkening clouds began to form in clusters within the sky, and lightning bolts along with thunder easily spooked the dog. He hid inside a doghouse as turmoil raged above. Then streams of water swept the can from its resting place toward a damaged gutter on the side of the house.

Weeks later, the homeowner discovered the can and tossed it into a recycling bin. At the recycling center, an employee pushed the can aside, since it had never been opened. She was unaware of imperceptible holes that slowly allowed a rotten substance to seep from inside. The can remained in a vacant building amongst hazardous substances, which later caused the facility to close. The building was left abandoned for months and became a site for delinquent youths to entertain themselves. They broke windows and wrote graffiti on the walls whenever they happened to skip school.

One day during their truancy, they were scared away. A very distraught black man peeped through an opening from one of the cracked windows. He was completely tired and beaten from the demonic spirit of addiction. He'd purposely scared them off so he could go to sleep. Earlier, he'd secured old boxes to fabricate a pallet in his quest for the oblivion of sleep. For him that cold dark building was as welcoming as a warm palace, for it sheltered him from the horrors of one more night.

The man woke the next morning from demanding pangs of hunger. Though his eyes watered from the glare of sunlight beaming through the window, he was able to focus and zoom in upon the can on a ledge. He retrieved a switchblade from the recess of his soiled sock, and it didn't take long for him to pry it open. But there wasn't much for him to consume, except thick residue inside the can.

Later, he found himself victorious over demons in his circles of life. He unwittingly killed himself consuming ptomaine poison.

A week later two old men smelled foul odors as they searched for copper within the building. Both were shaking terribly as they reported his body to the police.

Soon the official criminal investigation concluded. Gang members stripped the building of yellow tape and used it for expansion of their enterprise. Gang leaders chose to divide the main area of the building as an area for their girls to turn tricks. The girls had no problem making money, for they brought businessmen in and out the building steadily throughout the day.

After finding the jagged can, one of the younger boys used it for stashing drugs. He was robbed one day as he left the building, yet his drugs were well secured inside it. Devastated by his financial loss, the boy added chemicals, to increase the volume of his product, so he could make some extra cash.

Tipped off by a gas station attendant across the street, ATF agents raided the building and arrested everyone inside. One guy was shot by agents during his attempt to hide a gun along with cash inside a broken toilet.

The building didn't stay abandoned long. Soon an old man, middle-age woman, and teenage boy made it their home. Due to their lack of income, they dined on food extracted from the grocery store dumpster located in the area. Workers from the store thoughtfully packed unsellable food well enough for them to retrieve, which made the building occupants territorial. They would prevent others who lacked the necessities of life from occupying space.

One morning while rummaging, the old man found the can and decided to use it to panhandle. Usually he had enough money to purchase cigarettes and a bottle of liquor by the end of the day, which he didn't share with any other homeless people. One day, the middle-aged woman, after seeing him passed out, stole his bottle. Then she hastily emptied it and tucked it beneath his arm, hoping that when he awakened he'd believe he finished it himself.

The next day, they teamed up and panhandled for money. Both of them shuffled through the community collecting spare change in an old mug. They looked pathetic as they begged. Many people were not very sympathetic to giving change, offering food instead.

Nevertheless, they made ample enough money to purchase cigarettes singly, and the rest was spent on alcoholic beverages for them to make it through the night. They didn't mind sharing these hard-earned items with a teenager who'd just appeared.

The teenager was responsible for keeping a bonfire lit at night, for it was the break of winter. This eventually drew crowds of homeless people to take refuge in their building. And they congregated together like one big happy family.

A runaway, who happened to reside on the other side of the building, also gravitated to the fire. He didn't drink, but he had a bag of marijuana. He stumbled upon the can himself and thought it would be a good place to hide his weed when he went off to school.

Some were drinking and smoking during the day, while others waited to gather food from the soup kitchen or area dumpsters. By nighttime, they were all contented with being in a safe place for rest.

The chill of winter forced the three occupants to suspend former sentiments concerning others living in their building. They stood as silent symbols of invitation as now welcomed guests began to reside in their building. These new residents were contented standing in the soup kitchen line.

Several owners of businesses in that neighborhood complained to the mayor about the homeless living in that building. Their successful lobbying for its demolition resulted in the residents being on the streets once again.

The neighborhood children collected scraps from the building whenever they strolled through the neighborhood. One little girl became fascinated with her discovery of the mangled can on the vacant plot. She crushed it with her shoe until the can molded around her sole. She happily skipped all the way home, click-clacking on the sidewalk. Her mother, who was usually worried, was grateful when she came through the door with such a big smile upon her face.

"How was your day at school?" her mother asked.

The little girl replied, "It was fine."

"What did you learn?"

"Not much to talk about really. But on the way home, I learned a new sound of music."

"Can I hear it?"

"I don't think you want to go outside to hear it."

"Well, maybe you can tell me more about it after you wash up for dinner."

Later that night, after praying and tucking her little girl into bed, the mother noticed an old beat-up can beside the bed. She was disgusted at the sight of it, so she chucked the can in the recycling bin for early-morning pickup.

The little girl awoke that morning and sadly realized her can was missing, but didn't make a fuss about it. She rushed to school anxiously hoping to find something else meaningful in the rubbish.

The can finally made it to the incinerator. It was a grand time for that can. It was melted along with other aluminum objects and purified from all the mess it had been through. The stockperson once joked about it, saying, "If only that can could talk," and then he abandoned it.

Thinking its existence was worth nothing, the janitor had trashed it, and only the dog treasured it. Yet its deposit was much too shallow. The can had been passed through garbage, getting kicked around, and hit with a stick. It even came to its very stage of restoration, but again it was pushed along into further tribulations because it wasn't empty.

The can had apparently gone through a dreadful course of action. No one remembered its contents had initially been intended for good. It was banged up so badly throughout its journey, open wounds rotted away the sustenance inside. And the remaining contents had become so toxic, it caused a man to die.

After being long emptied of wholesome content, it still found forms of utilization. The old beat-up can became a safety net for drugs and a receptacle to solicit spare change. When surroundings for the can had fallen to dust, someone's little girl came along and remolded it to the sole of her shoe, and then it became the means for rejoicing and enjoyment. Slowly the can moved down the conveyor belt, and into the fire it went.

Those difficult times were necessary for that can to find its way to its final place of purpose. The can was taken away from all it endured to a place for ultimate transformation. It became a cornerstone for a foundation, which sat upon it a priceless jewel. The jewel was observed by those who beheld it through a protective glass cover. No one could afford it, yet everyone adored it, including the stockperson who'd first come into contact with it. The can had found its purpose.

*

I was so excited about writing this story. If a simple, everyday can could find purpose and affect so many lives, SO CAN I. I was so touched by the story that I decided to name it C.A.N., Ceasing All Negativity.

A little cookie to bite on:

Often due only to happenstance, one may find oneself in some remote place in life. The inherent potential of purpose is most definitely there; yet the ability for its demonstration is often stunted or shaped by directives of unforeseen tribulations. Thus, it often turns wholesome potential into toxic expressions of fatal negativity.

"But the God of all grace, who hath called us unto his eternal glory by Christ Jesus, after that ye have suffered a while, make you perfect, stablish, strengthen, settle *you*" (1 Peter 5:10 KJV).

What is in this message? Tribulation is defined as "a cause of great trouble or suffering." However, a perceived cause is not always true. Truth is that which conforms to reality; whereas, falsehood expressions are those which appear to be. Remember, "If life is but a stage and we are but actors upon it," then positive and negativity are dependent upon the audience doing the observing. Be not dismayed over circumstances in between scenes of life.

I believe there is a moment in life when we must wait along life's journey toward purpose for the final curtain to fall. We should be inspired by the motivating purpose of standing before The Ultimate Critic.

After spending a day fasting and praying, and laying prostate before the Lord, I heard a comforting spirit say, "Don't give up! Your story will be great; but I need you to release the hurt that caused you the most pain in your past—the scars, disappointments, and failures—then you can show others my power in you, and finally fulfill your purpose."

I thank God for giving me an ear to hear and for "Filtering It" for me.

Look at your past experiences! Can you see others influence upon how you are living? Do you believe in the power of change? Think of ways you CAN (cease all negativity).

_____
_____
_____
_____
_____
_____
_____
_____
_____
_____

"If we confess our sins, he is faithful and just to forgive us *our* sins, and to cleanse us from all unrighteousness" (1 John 1:9 NKJV).

ALISA D. BOYD

Chapter 3

A STATE OF CONFUSION BY IT

There is so much to tell, but I will only give you the highlights. As a young adult, my soul was thirsty for a spiritual anointing, although I'd ventured into a worldly lifestyle. I continually managed to visit churches, but there often seemed to be some disunity. If it wasn't commotional bickering over policy, it would be doctrinal errors spoken by the preacher; confusion and disorder in the church had become all too common.

Rev was the one who introduced me to the truth and reality of the unseen when I was a little girl. He invited me to personally strengthen my faith in The Most High God. I watched as he persevered in a labor of love. He had reconstructed a neighborhood skating rink on Gilsey Avenue, given to him by his brother, and turned it into a church. He worked diligently to build a place of praise and worship for the weary-hearted, the sick in spirit, and those lost in worldly passions.

His pursuit was like that of a doctor, for he often made emergency house calls on any given day, and would prescribe spiritual exercises or biblical scriptures for everybody who came to his tabernacle. It seemed as if he generated the sense of a holy place where all were compelled to discard their unholy lives. People's hearts were full of joy, peace, and happiness. Well, at least for the duration of the service.

One would get the feeling that spirits were destroyed and lives were restored with the service for the Lord that he strived to share with everyone. The atmosphere was this same way whether Rev married or buried a soul.

His calm and unchanging spirit left an imprint upon my mind. Life's sharp corners and rough edges were seen differently from behind the lenses of his meaningful life. His perspectives healed my broken heart and gave expansion to my core expectations. His discipline was with words having biblical foundations, no matter the situation presented.

I remember learning the following scripture that soothed my heart:

"Behold, I stand at the door, and knock: if any man hear my voice, and open the door, I will come in to him, and sup with him and he with me. To him that overcometh will I grant to sit with me in my throne, even as I also overcame and am set down with my Father in his throne. He that hath an ear, let him hear what the Spirit saith unto the churches" (Revelation 3:20-22 NKJV).

With Rev in my world, I was able to appreciate the true meaning of love, respect, appreciation, security, and support. Many times I found myself prodigal in situations. However, his memory in my walk or talk wasn't enough to keep me from squandering a righteous life away.

My spiritual quest was more challenging than running away from home at age eighteen and learning the streets. Messages of healing, due to worldly influences, blurred my vision of faith and hope. My wanting to escape from its grasp and being with the Lord were the only two things I desired.

Finding a way of escape became too challenging, so I continued pacifying myself with words from a voiceless expression of devastation. The more I wrote, the more soothing my thoughts became. Being loved was the missing component in my life, and one day I found words to articulate what I thought I'd lost from the following poem.

UNRAVELING AN EMOTIONAL BOND OF LOVE

Love does not force one to feel shameful
I had developed unlovable ways:
selfishness, a bad attitude,
and disgracefulness.

I questioned Love at every angle,
the Love I wanted,
the Love I needed, and the Love I desired.

Cheap talk about Love destroyed my destiny.
I confused flattery with Love.
I allowed this idea of Love to tear me down,
not understanding the constructive power
of its reality.

My feelings were devoid of Love when embraced.
I used false impressions of Love
to prey on others
whenever I was weak to the desires of my flesh.

My idea of Love was toxic,
therefore toxic relationships
became the essence
of my affairs.

My idea of Love was wrapped
in thoughts of numbness to its reality.

NOT CREATED TO BREAK

My awkward perception left me
wondering why family members
did not show true Love.

Yet it was I who truly did not understand it.
I thought Love divorced itself from me,
since life appeared to be
a hand dealt bad.

By grace and mercy, I later discovered that
Love is not something that can be shuffled.
It is something that can never
take partnership with weakness.

Love is too warm a feeling
to be silenced by numbness.
The spirit of Love began to unravel
the emotional bond I tied upon it.

When I made up my mind
to receive Love,
Love revealed to me
it was always there.

It dressed me in a gown of acceptance,
serenity and inspiration.
It led me down the isle of understanding to be
wed to the spirit of unity.

Stop for a moment and think about why unpleasant situations may occur in your life. Are you collecting spiritual tools necessary for you to handle those situations? Please express.

_____
_____
_____
_____
_____
_____
_____
_____
_____
_____
_____
_____

"My brethren, count it all joy when ye fall into divers temptations; Knowing [this], that the trying of your faith worketh patience. But let patience have [her] perfect work, that ye may be perfect and entire, wanting nothing" (James 1:2-4 KJV).

Chapter 4

BEGINNING TO MAKE SENSE OF IT

It didn't make sense to me. What am I to do? How should I feel? What is right? What is wrong? Rev had taught me the power of prayer, and that's what kept me going. I earnestly went to God in prayer:

Father, I need you. Please open my eyes so that I can see clearly what is before me. I am so confused. What am I supposed to think? I see the good and the bad all around me. However, I see Your handiwork getting clearer and clearer. I rejoice over the protective power You have given me as a little girl to keep my virginity when mindless boys tried to force me to give it up. I learned that there would be nothing to lose for those under Your grace and protection. I come to You now as a young adult asking you to uncover the mechanism of self-punishment that strips away my inner peace. It is that same mechanism which also destroys tenacity and sends me hopelessly wandering. Amen.

By the time I turned twenty-one, I woke up to find myself living in the heartless streets of Detroit, Michigan. I found myself in womanhood with no clear answers, and entering motherhood.

My old irresistible activities became less alluring no sooner than I accepted the role of a mother. I no longer felt comfortable indulging in pleasure-seeking activities and carelessness. The next five years, I found myself raising Brook and LeShawn, my two daughters, and a nephew Jigga as my son. The responsibility of raising my children at age twenty-six sent me seeking after answers from The Most High God.

The fear of vulnerability and the possibility of failure became mental vices that distorted my vision of having a better life. I needed those somehow hidden spiritual instructions that had been instilled in me by my grandparents. Deep within my spirit, I knew that God had never decreed me to be a failure. I just needed to hear Him better. By listening better, I could better receive His plan for grace. It must have been His grace and mercy that got me and the three children safely back to the place where I found my first spiritual connection in Dayton, Ohio.

Traveling with my three children from Detroit to Ohio was more peaceful than I'd imagined. The roads were safe, and I had no trouble getting pulled over by the police for driving above the speed limit. I made several trips from Ohio to Detroit, keeping the children connected with their family. Mechanical failure was something that always scared me, after getting stranded on the highway from my car running hot. It was a blessing to have roadside assistance when I got insurance on my car. It never fails!

There I was, driving in my Audi one day with just enough speed to creep into the embankment after stalling in the middle lane of the highway. As cars sped by blowing and showing no mercy, I began to think hard about where I could have ended up if someone had hit my car.

Sitting in my hot car waiting on a wrecker to tow my car made me think about burning in hell. I felt terrible, stranded on the side of the road, temperature blazing at 101 degrees. I didn't have to wait long to be rescued, but I never wanted to be in that predicament ever again. I thanked God for having mercy on me. Whenever I found myself headed down the wrong road, I looked to God for roadside assistance.

ALISA D. BOYD

A little cookie to bite on:

God's Will is that everyone will be delivered (saved) from sin and its consequences, which is death. This is called God's Plan of Salvation. There are several plans, but a simple one that is easy to understand is called "The Plan of Salvation." It consists of some scriptural verses, all from the Holy Bible starting with the book of Romans and the Gospel according to John, which explains the Plan of Salvation:

    (1) Who needs salvation

    (2) Why we need salvation

    (3) How God provides salvation

    (4) How we receive salvation

    (5) The results of salvation

    The steps are as follows:

Romans 3:10 KJV—"As it is written: There is none righteous, no, not one:"

Romans 3:23 KJV—"For all have sinned, and come short of the glory of God;"
    (Understand that all have sinned.)

Romans 5:8 KJV—"But God commendeth his love toward us, in that, while we were yet sinners, Christ died for us."

(Understand that The Most High God loves us anyway.)

Romans 6:23 KJV—"For the wages of sin *is* death; but the gift of God *is* eternal life through Jesus Christ our Lord."

(Know that sin results in death and hell; but The Most High God offers the gift of eternal life through Jesus.)

Romans 10:9 KJV—"That if thou shalt confess with thy mouth the Lord Jesus, and shalt believe in thine heart that God hath raised him from the dead, thou shalt be saved."

(Confess Jesus as Lord of my life and believe in my heart that The Most High God raised Him from the dead.)

Romans 10:13 KJV—"For whosoever shall call upon the name of the Lord shall be saved."

(Call upon the name of the Lord.)

Romans 10:17 KJV—"So then faith *cometh* by hearing, and hearing by the word of God."

(Accept the free gift of faith in Christ that comes by hearing the Word of The Most High God.)

OTHER SCRIPTURES:

John 3:16 KJV—"For God so loved the world, that he gave his only begotten Son, that whosoever believeth in him should not perish, but have everlasting life."

(Know that The Most High God loves us so much that He gave His son, Jesus, so that whosoever believes in, clings to, relies upon, and trusts in Him shall be saved.)

Acts 3:19 KJV—"Repent ye therefore, and be converted, that your sins may be blotted out, when the times of refreshing shall come from the presence of the Lord;"
>(Repent! Change direction. Turn away from sin and turn to Christ)

Ephesians 2:8-9 KJV—"For by grace are ye saved through faith; and that not of yourselves: [it is] the gift of God: Not of works, lest any man should boast."
>(Know that salvation is by The Most High God's grace "unmerited favor" and that there is no work that one can do to earn or receive The Most High God's free gift.)

John 14:6 KJV—"Jesus saith unto him, I am the way, the truth, and the life: no man cometh unto the Father, but by me."
>(Jesus said that He is the only Way to Heaven.)

Are you allowing the spiritual principle of life to free you from misunderstanding and "it's" issues in life? Are you embracing its power and rejecting the bond of personal feelings? Think of ways you can introduce someone today to this love you have inside.

___

"Jesus answered and said unto him, Verily, verily, I say unto thee, Except a man be born again, he cannot see the kingdom of God" (John 3:3 KJV).

Chapter 5

ACCEPTING LIMITATIONS OF IT

I endured countless moments of anger and thoughtlessness while trying to divert memories of physical abuse from invading my mindset. I was subjecting my children to certain levels of abuse that I'd received from Mother. I cussed and yelled at them, instead of speaking in a calm tone.

The fear of being confronted with past sins and shortcomings made me often isolate from others. I was not perfect. I lied and cheated, using men to provide me with luxuries the same way I saw men in my family using women to make them money. I also participated in notorious drug dealings. I escaped death far too many times.

Revisiting those type situations caused me to have panic attacks, along with stress and agony. I wanted freedom from issues that hindered me from having a relationship with The Most High God.

Emotional roadblocks stopped any advancement to recover my peace. Trusting little in The Spirit, and mostly in schemes, prevented me from getting out of bondage. I became terrified. I started to truly think I wasn't worthy to receive God's blessings.

Constructive meditations and holistic thoughts upon things vocalized at church compelled me out of depression. My fear was pacified by scriptures such as 2 Timothy 1:7 KJV. "For God hath not given us a spirit of fear, but of power, and of love, and of a sound mind."

I gained useful knowledge and a clearer understanding of those spiritual words which had been passed on from my grandparents. I got sick and tired of participation and solicitation in illegal activities with my family and male acquaintances.

I got to a point in my life where things became more visible to me. I realized that the ties I had from my bloodline, the non-productive ones, oppressed me. I put in a lot of negative work with my family, including picking up clients from the airport, laundering money, and storing drugs in my home.

But I was constantly fighting a war of lack. At twenty-eight, I ended up living in the same projects in which my grandparents raised their children. I reverted back to my childhood environment.

Living in the projects was not what I dreamed of for my children. Yet, I believe I had to go through that in order to break that curse off them and the generations to come. I made a mental note to stop agreeing with my adversaries and seek knowledge, wisdom, and understanding. I began to listen attentively to words spoken by one of my second cousins, who was the pastor of a Baptist church. My life became more focused on salvation and purpose after joining his church.

I've written Spoken Words from what I learned in the streets and how I analyzed them to taunt me when I was dealing with others.

ALISA D. BOYD

SPOKEN WORDS

People,

Does anyone value friendship?

Some call us their Cat – *a woman given to spiteful or malicious gossip; a small domesticated carnivore...*

Others call us their Dog – *bred in many varieties; characterized in the wild state...*

Companions called us their Boo – *used to express contempt or disapproval, to cry in derision, to show disapproval of.*

Homies call us their Nigga – *disparaging and offensive,* spoken way out of context

Such names given as if it holds high status: "Cat," "Dog," "Boo," and "Nigga."

Communicating with gestures from body movements, handshakes and snapping fingers...

Such limited language learned far from our roots.

What happened to companionship?

My Honey - *sweetness; pleasantness,*

My Sweetheart - *one who is loved...*

My Baby – *a person of whom one is deeply fond...*

Where are the morals instilled by principles from our bloodline?

"Yes, Sir" and "Yes, Ma'am" or "No, Sir" and "No, Ma'am"

When will we see the diabolical message?

Intellect stunted by slang words is not a cultural myth.

Pride and a feel for maturity are often contaminated by false hopes.

Minds destroyed; drunk and high off alcohol and drugs and anything else in the streets.

Obviously, what we really needed was a hug and true love.

People,

We are often blinded by the enemy, with no understanding of the abuse from drugs and alcohol.

Drugs and alcohol distort the reality, of things that once made sense.

Careless attitudes are poisonous opinions of the mind.

Conversations using Morse code, exposing what can be found in secrets.

Being ghetto fabulous was once established to bring a destructive element into our cultural status.

Sleazy clothing, senseless fighting, stupid comments and

thoughtless actions are fruitless.

Bickering words used out of context cause chaos and should not be your new norm.

People,

We must stop playing games and telling half of the truth, and then say, "It's reality!"

We must stop justifying the sinful abominations of sexual gratification with the term "generational curse!"

We must stop letting self-imposed limitations become the glass ceiling above our spiritual awareness.

We must stop allowing an imposed history of hopelessness and low self-esteem "hold our purpose captive."

We must stop adopting fragmented images and learn to love ourselves.

Stop and think...

                    True LOVE is a gift

Today, are you affirming positive words when communicating with others? Be more creative with the people you surround yourself with and stop blaming others for your mistakes.

_____

"Ye are of God, little children, and have overcome them: because greater is he that is in you, than he that is in the world" (1 John 4:4 KJV).

Chapter 6

SPEAKING VICTORY OVER IT

I made every attempt to exemplify and represent the being that God decreed me to be, by following that inner voice encouraging me to go back to school. It was challenging of course, yet receiving an associate's degree in business management from Sinclair Community College was a step toward changing my life. Becoming a valuable servant to others through The Spirit of The Most High God gradually became my pleasure, passion, and pain.

However by the time I turned thirty-six, I began to struggle raising three children as a single mother. The toughest situation I'd encountered during that period was due to many conflicting interests. After earning my degree in business management, I took my oldest daughter to get a babysitting certificate through the Red Cross. I began working at Miami Valley Hospital and stayed there for two years. Being steadfast in prayer, I believe, landed me employment with Emory Worldwide Airlines. My oldest daughter watched the younger two children for two hours after school until I got home from work.

I had no idea my children had gotten so far out of control; the younger two were skipping school, getting kicked off the school bus, and showing out in class. We spent many days in the psychologist's office seeking therapy for their disruptive behaviors, over which I had no control. My youngest daughter was diagnosed with a chemical imbalance and prescribed medication. She made note that her behavior was enticed by her brother. My little girl worshipped the ground her brother walked on and would do anything for him.

These concerns led to heart-wrenching options of either letting go of Jigga, or allowing the system to dismantle my whole family. How could I live without having Jigga close to me? I raised my nephew Jigga as my son for ten years, and he was just as meaningful to my story of life as my breath of life. That dreaded day became unavoidable. I reached out to his paternal family members, and no one was in the position to raise him.

Jigga's playing with a clothes iron and leaving third degree burns on LeShawn alarmed Children's Services. We had apparently all flunked our counseling sessions, and the counselors weren't satisfied with the reports from school. No matter how much I cried, the counselors considered Jigga's burning my younger daughter on the back as a major mental and social breakdown. So with dignity and a thorough sense of powerlessness, I had no other choice but to reluctantly hand him over to the same authorities that found placement for my sister's other children.

My family was torn apart by the system, and I thought a regimen of pills for anxiety and depression would be the solution to make the nightmares go away. I was utterly mistaken. It was only through prayer, and my forgiveness of others that strength arrived to help me move forward.

The Most High God had very strange ways of teaching me acceptance of my limitations. I learned there will always be a negative and a positive to most things in life, that I couldn't save the whole world.

That wonderful experience at Emory Worldwide Airlines lasted only a year. Being laid off was difficult, especially after I'd purchased a new car. However, it was not long before I landed another job at a startup charter school.

My mind became over-occupied with helping other children after being blessed with a job at Colin Powell Leadership Academy as the EMIS (Education Management Information System) coordinator. I labored day and night with training and recruitment. I recruited my dearest cousin Doreen to be a teacher's aide. I also brought on board my goddaughter's father as a computer technician. I asked another relative, to fill in as the school nurse. My uncle's ex-girlfriend was one of the bus drivers, and I also brought on two teachers from my children's previous school. Doreen and I also added a very successful before- and after-school program.

Doreen seemed as passionate for helping children as I. It could honestly be said that The Most High God gave us the fire to put that school on the map. We were young single mothers inspired by what we could add to the lives of at-risk youth. We labored long hours assisting with getting the foundation laid. We passed out flyers in surrounding projects inviting youth to attend the charter school. With assistance from Doreen's family, we went to Cincinnati and picked up donated furniture. We painted the furniture in time for Open House. Doreen and I financially assisted parents with purchasing uniforms.

One time, I was just days away from adopting a newborn baby boy. He was part of a sibling group awarded to the court that I helped get registered in school. The adoption was not granted because a social worker deemed it a conflict of interest, due to my relationship with the biological mom.

In spite of all the hard work done, my contract ended unexpectedly at the end of the school year. No renewal was forthcoming due to irreconcilable differences with my salary. Yet, no matter how bad situations got, I seemed to always bounce back. The Spirit appeared to connect me to the most relevant scriptures, which in turn convinced my heart to accept things I couldn't see.

"And it shall come to pass, if ye shall hearken diligently unto my commandments which I command you this day, to love the LORD your God, and to serve him with all your heart and with all your soul" (Deuteronomy 11:13 KJV).

I heard a voice say, "It's time to take a walk with God and move away from Ohio." I had gotten used to taking risks, although I never anticipated moving out of town so suddenly. I believed that voice to be a spiritual directive. So I obediently packed up and moved forward. I began to see bad experiences, including my contract ending, as a test of my faith. I went in prayer for that ordeal.

Lord, please open my heart and mind to clearly see the meaning behind the times when I was broken, crushed, and grieved. At the same time, I felt that I was being set aside by You, being gently pushed into an anointing so that I may further walk into the path of Your purpose and my destiny. I know it was You who sent me into that office to tell my ex-employers, "I forgive you for treating me and my children like garbage." Thank you, Lord, for giving me a spirit of forgiveness. Amen.

My cousin Franklin put his life's agenda on hold to assist my move to Georgia. Extending the invitation to my cousin was not what The Spirit had instructed me to do. I easily fell back into my former way of thinking and suspended my trust in God. I instantly put trust in my cousin to make it to the top. Franklin was known for being prosperous, but his resources became too risky for me. I needed a much stronger foundation to survive the next few years in Georgia.

Anxiety controlled my mind. I was unable to make any sound decisions. Accepting reality in a cognitive way was common to me. I displaced my feelings of impending failure by gaining fragments of success through manipulating people. I pointed the finger at Franklin when resources weren't readily accessible to start a business. Franklin made it easy for me to blame him for failed accomplishments. I ran him away after taking his kindness for weakness.

I often got in traps that only the Spirit of The Most High God could rescue me from. Brook and LeShawn, my two angels, were weary victims of my lack of discretion and lustful heart. I spent many nights bargaining and begging God to change my disposition. One night, I received revelation from The Spirit. It commanded me to get rooted in a home church before the ramifications of my sinful nature destroyed me completely.

As a child, I had been taught to be repentant and be humble, which gave me liberty to choose my own spiritual direction and behavioral therapy. What I needed most was deliverance from the compulsiveness of sin and reconciliation with The Spirit of The

Most High God. Fulfilling the command to get rooted in a church wasn't as taxing to my mind as the idea of finding the right one. I often reflect upon that pilgrim-like journey that led me drifting in and out of churches.

The open-hearted choice I made to adhere to the Word of The Most High God changed my life drastically. I began to receive freedom from flesh-toned passions, as I read scriptures before going to bed. The Spirit seemed to tap into my brain and release the flood of burdens and heaviness. It was a good enough feeling to make me further submit to The Spirit of God.

Biblical scriptures of encouragement filtered throughout my heart and freed my mind from bondage. I developed a "vision board" to help guide me to my future. I read inspirational books and limited my time watching television. At one point, I was consumed by the spirit of soap operas, but I had to understand the value of abstaining from negative conversations. The Holy Spirit guided me to surrender my life wholeheartedly to the Lord.

In preparation for Sunday morning, I laid three halter dresses on my bed and contemplated which would be appropriate for church. LeShawn and Brook were excited because we were to revisit a mega church. They tended to their hygienic obligations and scrambled to put on their matching sundresses.

My enthusiasm changed while driving through traffic. I was irritated by people carelessly speeding to get a last-minute parking space. My thoughts go scientific sometimes when irrational situations occur. I needed some type of anchor to hold me down and manage the adrenaline flowing through my body; I could almost hear it.

A high level of dopamine was saturating my brain, preparing me for mortal combat. I managed to calm my nerves from the ten-minute traffic rush, once the car was parked. I had projected myself mentally into the power of the service, and what can be more peaceful than that?

The girls were intrigued by the enormous size of the church. The view was much better than our first visit. We followed a crowd up the stairway and made our way into the balcony. I counted each row in the second level of the balcony. We sat on the third row in seats four, five, and six. I peered through the congregation witnessing thousands of people seated. The beautiful structure and atmosphere of the church was amazing.

I observed women dressed in stylish clothes and fancy hats. Others came dressed down. A thought crossed my mind. *Are these men and women really sincere about their worship, or are they looking to hook up with someone in the congregation, or maybe even the pastor?*

Negative thoughts re-entered my mind as I watched the congregation offered their tithes. I reflected back upon my limitations and seeming inability to prosper. A signal transmitted thoughts into my thalamus (the part of the brain that monitors and processes information). I listened attentively to hear if the preacher was leaning toward his own understanding on how to live, along with his personal depiction of the Bible.

A circuit shorted in my brain, distancing me from my carnal mind. Back in the day, I would have shouted, "Ol' boy got it going on up in here."

The cerebral cortex (the outer part of my brain) had been jolted by the Spirit of The Most High God and brought to my remembrance that I was sent by divine orders. The Spirit opened my heart and mind for deliverance. The pastor's message about life held my attention, and with all due respect, I had to admit the anointing appeared to be all over him.

The pastor's deliverance of the message stimulated my spiritual mindset. The message preached that day was not from the average man. His message removed the feeling of guilt and shame I'd carried for several weeks.

I was very familiar with that type of discipline. Rev used to chastise me with scriptures to that magnitude. No longer could I run from the fact of being involved with a married man.

I sat in my seat weeping and promised God I would stop seeing that man. The Spirit of The Most High God pulled me back together through a solemn prayer. The pastor was well received, and that experience taught me not to judge or criticize people based on past experience.

I went back the next Sunday and was impressed by the way people ran, jumped, screamed, and shouted throughout the church. They appeared to be genuinely filled with the Holy Spirit. That service had me feeling like a new creature.

I was on the rebound from ending a toxic relationship that stained my character, plagued my determination to succeed, and weakened my ability to overcome great obstacles. Nevertheless, the dopamine level in my brain wasn't high enough to compel a total surrender to God. My sinful nature kept me at arm's length from the full commitment that I chose not to make. I was determined to personally take care of what I viewed as my intimate needs in the way I knew best. I had a colorful history of keeping a man on the rebound as my safety net for emotional needs.

I was now thirty-seven years old. My idle time was spent with Kenny, the other guy, to pacify my intimate needs. Kenny was an amazing guy. He worked at the post office and drove a nice Mercedes. I parlayed at his house while he played music on his baby grand piano. I felt obligated to satisfy his ego and made sure there wasn't any chaos during our weekend rendezvous. Arguing was not permitted and there were no conversations pressuring him to attend church. That courtship kept me content, but it ended abruptly when I got news that my mother had a mild heart attack.

Moving Mother away from Dayton, Ohio seemed to be a great opportunity to build a mother-and-daughter relationship. I prayed excessively, asking The Most High God to strengthen our relationship. Nevertheless, it was Mother's unpredictable behavior and my desire to control things outside my power that launched me into a world full of uneasiness, unhappiness, shame, and guilt.

Somehow, The Most High God took pity upon me and directed my mind away from my past with the scripture "He giveth power to the faint; and to *them that have* no might he increaseth strength" (Isaiah 40:29 KJV).

I soon reflected upon a sermon stating that mothers and daughters were going to be reconnected. I had high expectations of Mother restoring her health and gaining a better outlook on life. Being in her presence put me in a cheerful state of mind. I was grateful she was very much alive and in possession of a stable mind, especially after all she had been through.

God had given us permission to experience more tomorrows and move forward, but as always, the devil had another plan. The enemy stood by, using every device to sabotage our relationship. I welcomed Mother with open arms upon a red carpet, so to speak, unwittingly inviting the opportunity for dark spirits of dissension and malice to enter the equation.

Mother kicked a heroin habit that seemed, to me, to last almost twelve years. She later developed a stronger dependency on cigarettes and alcohol. I stopped smoking cigarettes, hoping it would influence her to stop as well. Personal objectives between us drew a wedge when I stopped supplying cigarettes.

I was never addicted to any openly celebrated drugs; mine was a hidden illness. The disease in my brain craved the need for sexual gratification. The infection started when I was nine years old. My brother, protector, and friend was struggling with his own demons. He was fully into puberty and lost balance with his sexual nature, and I became victim to its symptoms.

My body eventually craved the feeling for sick affection, and I was no longer immune to it. This was my addiction, so I began to embrace it. Unwholesome sex, spirit-depriving sex, and undesirable sex became the cure-all to my emotional problems in life. Yet due to its dark origin, I was afraid to shed light of my shameful illness with anyone

Do you believe there is a brighter future for your tomorrow? Have you taken the time to acquaint yourself with The Spirit of The Most High? Can you talk about those unwholesome deeds and emotional situations?

_____

_____

_____

_____

_____

_____

_____

_____

_____

"According to my earnest expectation and *my* hope, that in nothing I shall be ashamed, but *that* with all boldness, as always, *so* now also Christ shall be magnified in my body, whether *it be* by life, or by death" (Philippians 1:20 KJV).

NOTES

Chapter 7

DELIVERANCE FROM IT

It was guilt and shame that always sent me running to church for comfort. My strength in The Spirit of The Most High God became connected to the ministry at a megachurch. The scriptural expounding suppressed my mind and heartfelt sexual desires.

The change in my life came when the power of the Spirit began to caress my soul, mind, and body from the inside out. I began to glorify the healing power of His Word. I didn't care about the way I clapped my hands or moved my feet; a supernatural force grabbed hold of my mind, allowing me to hear an utterance extremely different from the pastor's voice.

The power transmitted through those utterances had true authority to restore me from all aspects of victimization, and from that unconscious penchant for self-destruction.

It was favor from The Most High that extended the key to initiate my spiritual release. I no longer feared the syndrome of a dead woman walking. I realized the Spirit of deliverance is truly for everyone. At one time I believed it was impossible for me to be delivered and set free, but I found a constant companion in that very Spirit.

I accepted my call to salvation and joined New Birth Missionary Baptist Church with my two daughters. I reconnected my soul to a spirit created before I'd entered Mother's womb. The pastor encouraged me to believe in the Spirit I'd concealed from myself all those years. I re-discovered the love of the "Spirit" of Christ sealed inside of me. And I didn't entertain Mother's voice, or talk from other relatives discouraging me from being part of a megachurch. Rather than being persuaded by people, I chose to operate under what I believed to be obedience.

I studied scriptures and prayed fervently. I understood the concept of renewing my mindset in order to live a kingdom-like life. I refused to be torn by the grip of guilt from my past. The Spirit of The Most High God helped me walk into a new season. Attending Wednesday night Bible Study and Sunday morning worship services helped consolidate my devotion to God. I praised Him continuously for showering upon me His grace and mercy.

After six months of searching for employment, I was blessed with a job offer two days before Christmas, with DeKalb County Treasury and Accounting, as an accounting tech/auditor. There I faced unpleasant encounters with my coworkers only the Spirit working through me could fix. Yet, because of my love for God, I learned how to love people unconditionally and not take things to heart.

I received spiritual revelation, but my nature still struggled against submitting to God's authority. I repeatedly recited the words from Philippians 4:13 KJV: "I can do all things through Christ which strengtheneth me."

That scripture reference was taken for granted. My trust was with the person in the pulpit praying. I ran to every altar call. One day, the pastor ministered to us to pray over one's own self, directing everyone to take his spiritual growth to a higher level. I also learned the dangers of feeding into my weaknesses.

What I found to have empowered me most was the information received on fasting and praying. I recognized that my spiritual maturity increased during a corporate fast for twenty-one days with one meal per day. My consistency of this practice along with its effect upon my demeanor displeased those in league with the enemy. The devil, also known as the father of lies, used my family as tools to oppress me. Through listening and learning, I subdued the attack of the enemy by uttering scriptures from the Bible. I began fasting and praying on my own for three days at a time and often continued for up to seven days.

The collectiveness of the Spirit, due to not eating or drinking on my twenty-four-hour fast, caused my spiritual awareness to be so hallowed, I felt as if I had become a church. I loved God in the way I perceived Jesus to speak of the church as His bride.

I often reminded myself that my move to Atlanta in August 2002 was in hopes of making a drastic change in my life. One thing I wanted the most was for Daddy to see I was making positive accomplishments, but that never happened. Two months after I bought my house in September 2003, I received a phone call to come to Ohio as soon as possible. Daddy went into a coma the day before Thanksgiving in 2003. He was on life support, and the tests showed large percentage of alcohol in his body.

In the midst of packing my clothes for the trip, I thought about some of the great accomplishments in his lifetime. He'd helped raise Mother's three children when they met, and moved us to California to make a better life when my younger sister and little brother were born. Detroit had left me with many scars, but I remember Daddy had always tried to provide for us. Years after we'd moved back to Dayton, Ohio, he eventually got himself clean. He'd also encouraged me to do my best during my high school years.

Daddy had a strong will to be a provider for the family, and he wanted to have a close relationship with his grandchildren. It appeared to me that he had given my family all he had to give. His time was up, and there was nothing more left in him to give us. I believe he may have experienced most things he wanted in life, unlike many others who never saw their dreams come true.

Those thoughts made it easy for me to give my approval for the doctor to pull the plug. I helped with the arrangements for his funeral, although I did not attend his home-going on Monday, December 8, 2003, due to a disturbance with my little sister.

I immediately made an attempt to re-establish a relationship with my biological father. I begged him to visit my home, although inviting him to Georgia brought back the bad memories of when I'd reached out to him as a teenager.

But I learned to love him without trying to fix him. Every attempt I made to let go of the pain and the hurt from my childhood seasoned me to see the joy of living. I explained how I loved him more than he ever knew. Yet, I must admit, I wasn't sure if I had enough forgiveness in my heart for him trying to use me to make a drug deal.

It was less than a year from the time Daddy had died when I got a call from my brother Andrew, this time telling me our biological father had just died. We celebrated his home-going on November 22, 2004, three days before Thanksgiving. Those trips back to Ohio were not the least bit pleasant, but the Holy Spirit helped me learn how to grieve unexpected deaths.

Every time I prepared myself to attend a funeral, I thought of Rev's home-going in 1987, one of the saddest days I ever endured.

*

I felt a spirit of defeat take control of me when I got the news about Rev collapsing at church service during the Thanksgiving holiday. I couldn't hold it together long enough to see the casket close on that Saturday afternoon on December 19th. Nor could I bear going to the burial at the National Cemetery for Veterans.

I held a strong disappointment toward God for taking Rev at a time when his guidance was much needed. I accepted no explanation for his death. I was brutally upset with God. My broken heart cut into anyone that came close. I subjected myself to dangerous drug dealings with my relatives. Everyone in that family unit seemed to be jacked up, and had lost respect for life.

As it is written, there is a purpose and a season for everything, and the foundation for this had been laid in eternal past by The Most High God's infinite plan. It so happens to be that several monumental paternal figures in my life shared the same season of departure. They all left a void within my world around or immediately after Thanksgiving. Every time the tradition was to be observed, I found myself unconsciously or consciously embracing clouds of gloom. What was I to be thankful about when the gift of giving had been abruptly changed to taking? My source of spiritual guidance—taken; my blueprint of stability and structure—taken; my genetic whipping boy to direct my mixed emotions also was taken during the Thanksgiving season.

*

After all those years, I was still grieving Rev's death. I idolized Rev. He was the only "real man" I knew for a long time. His characteristic of a true family man plagued my heart, because I worshipped him instead of The Most High God. He healed the brokenness from sins that sullied my heart, and we had an inseparable bond.

From time to time, I also called him Daddy. I appreciated seeing Rev live his life according to the words he preached. He truly loved God and people. He operated under an anointing to win souls to Christ. His life came to an end without warning. He passed out at his church, was rushed to the hospital, and lay in a coma for weeks. Facing Rev's death wasn't easy, and being in denial invited an unclean spirit to reside in my mind.

It took a lot for me to reacquaint my life with the Word of God. Church service inspirations were not the same for me when Rev made his transition home. The evil spirits within my dreadful dreams were no longer fettered by his gripping sermons. They were eager to get re-acquainted with me, and made much haste while coming back to haunt me. The churches I visited didn't give me the feeling of sanctuary that I once sought, and I couldn't find that place of refuge to suppress chaotic emotions and those feelings of being unloved.

When I finally surrendered to God, I found two churches in Dayton that elevated me. But my unwillingness to suppress my issues caused me to transgress upon the will of God. It appeared as if I was forfeiting what was to be received by His decree, until I chose to allow His will to be fulfilled. Whenever I allowed the Spirit to manifest within and outside myself, while facing issues, I was able to see most dangers before me.

When I joined the megachurch, I gained hope and had less fear. I was criticized by many people, and it was those criticisms that changed my life. I prayed for direction and discernment, chasing after the love of God. The power received from the Spirit of God allowed me to open my eyes to challenge things I was formerly too afraid to confront.

It appeared that God's plan for me was to be instrumental in ending generational destruction from demonic influence that ran rampant within my family. It was an appointed time to bind demonic spirits that hindered me.

What was prescribed for me by the Spirit required confrontation with many issues I didn't want to handle alone. I prayed for God to deliver me from my issues.

I anticipated that the directives concerning those issues would come through the pastor; I was wrong. The Spirit put forth an elder from the offspring of Dr. King to minister those directives to me. There was no doubt a potentially endless flow of wisdom and knowledge was to be obtained that day. I felt as if the Spirit of grace compelled the elder's heritage of leadership, foresight, and truthfulness to be blanketed over me.

I listened attentively as it was discussed how to overcome "it" issues that hardened one's mind, body, and soul. There were very many issues that distorted and restricted my choice to fully embrace the Spirit of The Most High God.

The most prominent issue within was the dominating aspect of my being inappropriately touched as a child. My being was mentally shattered. Due to that childhood trauma, it was then easier to deal with life, pretending that I didn't know what was going on.

The elder explained the nature of socially traumatized youth, implying that these children dealt with issues that should not have been intended for them. I gratefully opened my heart to adhere to the Word of God. Psychological walls tumbled down as the Spirit boldly revived my skeletons. I became re-acquainted with a part of life that I had banished to a far and remote place. My once dry bones bristled in front of me, refreshed with life.

One of my siblings used to make annoying sexual advances toward me repeatedly, but I'd never said anything to anybody. The Webster dictionary defines this as "molestation." Yet the act became mutual. Why did I become a willing participant in an inappropriate sexual act and secrecy? I fed into it because I was scared to talk about it. Who was going to listen to me? Besides, I saw my little sister being molested, and no one had talked about that. Could I have been taught to hide my trauma? Yes, this was "my trauma." It was not an act of children being curious.

My brother had been introduced to having sex with an older woman, so we both were victimized by the spirit of molestation. I often had flashbacks of what took place, which caused me to have ongoing problems with relationships and my self-esteem.

Being able to pray about it wasn't easy. I had to pray for understanding and be comfortable with what was revealed to me. Then I asked, "Why did it happen to me?"

That answer did not come right away. So I continued to hold on to my emotions and began seeing more flaws within myself. One day, I unexpectedly heard a voice say, "The trauma you went through in life happened so you can give God glory."

I had been through a lot, but letting that go was my biggest challenge. I gave God the glory, and instantly I felt trauma-free. The ultimate step I had to make was to believe I was set free.

It's unfortunate that people are judged for speaking out years after a traumatic event. It's even worse when people lie about being abused. It took over thirty years for me to heal. I praise God publicly for allowing my brother and me to talk about it, and move past it. He discussed things with me I never knew happened to him. At one point, I questioned if he needed counseling, concerned that he had suffered from a mental breakdown caused by the memories of being seduced by his molester.

I felt my brother's sincerity when he apologized. Although, the most important thing was for him to believe I had sincerely forgiven him. Neither of us should be defined by the trauma we suffered. I offered my forgiveness and prayed that he forgive the person who seduced him.

The Spirit safely exposed things from a worldly view that were openly meant to physically, spiritually, mentally, and emotionally destroy me. Though the Spirit of God rendered them powerless over me, I must admit, they still scared me to death.

My heart palpitated as images of perversion within my family refracted upon the windows of my soul. I saw past the bruises and gravitated to women turning tricks with men for cash. That's why growing up as a child was so difficult. I mimicked what others were doing, and those things began to make sense.

The elder's statement, "Learn to deal with your 'It' issues," was a very therapeutic clause in the message that helped deal with my pain. I stopped using my body and my cunning ways as a tool to get money. I also stopped doing other unrighteous behaviors that I'd witnessed others doing—cussing, smoking, drinking alcohol, and entertaining non-productive people.

The elder's message helped me see spiritual dynamics in God's principle of unconditional love. I was given a panoramic assessment of being separated from my parents. My slipping into traps, my wandering away from spiritual training, as well as the influence of my grandparents, could not be ignored. Various aspects of unconditional love were demonstrated by my grandparents. Their prayers and teachings kept me covered by the promises of Jesus. I realized my spiritual relationship with them was aligned by the will of God.

My first physical traits of love known as "eros," or romantic love, came from a childhood sweetheart, Michael, during my freshman year in high school. No matter what takes place between me and my siblings, no one could ever take away the "storge," or familial love, for both my biological father's children by different women and my siblings from Mother. The "philia," or friendship as a kind of love, I gained the last years in high school when I met my boss' son Jessie and later in life with Mr. Ron, is a level of love I have learned to appreciate between two people.

Yet I will forever be grateful and hold on strong to the "agape," or selfless love or charity, shown by my grandparents, who nurtured me and guided me for the betterment of my life.

The elder's voice seemed to single me out with an enlightening health-check. The Spirit had peculiar ways of making me take notice of my issues. This time, it was by way of a hard-hitting element that weakened my body and caused tremendous pain.

A cyst had broken and entered the cavity of my womb. The cyst, like most criminals, had destroyed my peace. It assaulted, and battered its way around, my ovaries. The pain in my body restricted my mobility. The cyst's criminal trespass daily robbed my body of strength and left evidence of pain each month during my menstrual cycle.

I listened carefully to what the Lord communicated into my spirit. I couldn't redeem parts of my destiny that I'd unwittingly made void due to risky behaviors. I thought my problems as a young adult could be resolved with limitless sex, countless money, bottomless alcohol, and ceaseless drug deals.

Pain medicine was a quick cure to soothe my careless "incidents." I initiated regulated use of birth control pills, retaining only a minimal cache of condoms. I was sent to the clinic because of my ungodly escapades. As a result of this, I killed a special part of my dreams.

The Spirit kept the elder's sermon simmering within my conscience. I made it convenient to be stewed in the pot of tests and trials that the enemy cooked up for me. I allowed false accusations to deeply hurt me, and my efforts spent upon vindication stirred me away from the Spirit.

My eyes were eventually pried open. I was allowed to foresee imminent dangers and abort further travels down a deadly road. The self-destructive choices I'd made in life had been triggered by my environment.

My expressed behaviors were influenced by those dark forces of fornication, lust, and promiscuity. I had no concern about my self-image. I was attracted to worthless companionships. I had no discretion, and my body was a tool used to obtain passion with every attempt to avoid pain. In my mind, I had no identity.

My issues were formed into a fortress for me to retreat behind, where I saw no shame, heard no shame, and felt no shame. I had one foot in and one foot out of the grave, and entertaining soul-stifling people became common. It was God's mercy that kept me alive. The elder made a profound declaration for me to deal with all those issues.

The soul-reviving words I received from the elder transmitted good news into my spirit, mind, and heart. My spirit and mind was put into position to accept why I had to deal with issues from the past.

The joy at that moment stirred me to those same feelings I felt toward my grandparents, who, I believe, were the most righteous people on earth. They'd introduced me to various expressions of love for the Lord. But never did they discuss the issue of demonic generational transfers.

I think the effects of those transfers were clear to them because they appeared to be cemented in our family's background. Is it possible they had the wisdom to know that some things, when brought to light, may contaminate and destroy the observer?

The elder pointed out how some bloodlines perpetuate curses within them. Thoughts of sexual abuses endured by my mother, brother, sister, and daughter taunted me. These awful experiences in our lives seemed to support my belief that all social encounters, whether godly or ungodly, were a part of life, that my family background sealed any option for doubt.

The elder continually spoke with conviction, and the Spirit

provided me with a platform to observe why angry spirits easily invaded my body. The absence of any relationship after the introduction to Ken, my biological father, had left me very insecure at the age of seven. Accepting parental directives from my stepfather at that point was difficult.

Mother kept a distance between me and Ken. However, an interrupted experience triggered my emotions when I was eighteen years old. I was then old enough to see Ken without Mother's permission. I was hoping the opportunity would inspire Ken to establish an enriched relationship between us. But instead, he chose for this opportunity to enrich his pockets. Ken bartered away our relationship with the idea of selling me to a South American kingpin as the means to sweeten a drug deal.

I would've done anything to have a relationship with Ken, until I realized he wanted me to have sex with a complete stranger. Who would have ever thought my own biological father wanted to pimp me to get a good price on a kilo of cocaine? Not going through with his plan drew a wedge between us, and the anger I felt from that experience caused me to disown him for many years.

I really didn't want to mentally relive that situation, but it was necessary in order to adequately observe the occurrences in my childhood. I needed to identify and expose the cause of pain in order for me to move forward.

"Am I able to forgive my father for exposing me to sex trafficking?" I questioned.

The elder then uttered, "Say no to the devil trying to control thoughts in your mind."

So with that being said, I instantly forgave my father.

The strengthening Spirit of God prepared my heart to accept the most painful event of my life. Evil spirits of depression quickly tormented the innermost part of my mind when Rev passed out at the church I watched him reconstruct. Darkness fell upon my world along with feelings of hurt and loneliness when he died.

Being intoxicated with grief and no direction for resentment, I disrespectfully believed The Most High God did not give Rev a fair chance. My reckless, sinful, and unrighteous living during the aftermath of his death made it clear that the Gospel of Christ had been rejected from my heart. And I maintained a standard of doing wrong and had little or no regard to what others thought about my behavior.

Saying no to the devil during that service helped remove the anger he sowed in my mind. Soon I began to relate more to the dynamics of spiritual gain. I was being delivered from the hurtful feeling of Ken not being there in my life. I was being refreshed from the stifling lack of understanding due to a Mother's abrasive love.

Last but not least, I was given enough healing to live with an open wound, which was the loss of Rev.

I understood that holding on to those issues would hinder me from becoming the woman God created me to be. That service helped me learn how to walk with the Spirit of Understanding.

After all those years, I began to finally recognize aspects of my life's plan according to "the divine scheme of things." I sat in my seat with tears streaming, releasing the pain from guilt. I was so ashamed of my affiliations with drug dealers and murderers. I was determined to make up for all those years lost as a child and young adult. The chambers in my heart slowly became unclogged.

At the closing of that sermon, my once-expired spirit had been revived by the power of the Holy Spirit.

The elder reminded me that God had a grace period, and that time, along with circumstances, was part of the blueprint of His divine purpose. I wept with joy and began thanking the Spirit for breaking the enemy's stranglehold on my mind, heart, and soul. I realized it was predestined for me to be confronted with my issues. It was never intended for me to live an unrighteous lifestyle. I was to be an overcomer.

I went home thinking about the damage I had done by unrighteous living. The clarity received from the Spirit presented me with vivid pictures of situations I was to overcome. The eternal power of the Spirit stripped away the vice of prescription painkillers and anxiety pills, and lifted me up and above a diseased mind of sexual lewdness.

Yes, the Spirit had freed me from corrupt passions of the flesh through renewal of my spirit. My slate was being wiped clean, and instantly the enemy no longer appeared to be controlling my mind.

Are you living your life based on how you can achieve worldly possessions? Do you have an excessive desire for material things and money, and gain them dishonestly? Think of some ways you can change your lifestyle to live honorably.

_____

_____

_____

_____

_____

_____

_____

_____

_____

"Let your conversation be without covetousness; and be content with such things as ye have: for he hath said, I will never leave thee, nor forsake thee. So that we may boldly say, The Lord is my helper, and I will not fear what man shall do unto me" (Hebrews 13: 5-6 KJV).

Chapter 8

BRINGING CLOSURE TO IT

My inner turmoil and the deceptive feeling of betraying my brother Andrew, rather than exposing social ills that victimized both of us, caused me high levels of hatred for sick secrets. It was not easy for me to accept the fact that it was my choice not to tell what happened between my brother and me. That ordeal caused me to feel inadequate. I wasn't sure if a man could ever truly love me. It was much easier for me to make a living conning men out of money. I'd made a choice just as well to sway away from my grandparents' teaching and acquaint myself with luxury cars, exotic animals, expensive clothes, nice jewelry, and drugs.

Taking responsibility for my wrongdoing was necessary in order for me to address my issues; it almost had me depressed. Yet the Spirit of Grace transformed my mind as I sought to look back on life as a teenager.

I had a full-time job at eighteen and was blessed with owning a new car. I paid my car notes on time and had a good credit rating. It appeared as if I was reaping rewards for showing my elders respect and helping others. It later became clear to me that those were first fruits from the harvest of my wise decisions, and this helped stimulate my growth above childhood issues.

My positive energy dwindled away when I rejected instructions from Mother, who gave me some great advice as a teenager, clearly warning me about getting corrupted by our family. Receiving instructions from Mother had never been easy due to the limited affection she displayed. At one point, she banned me from hanging out with my cousins. But I ran away from home to hang out with them.

Yes, Mother was right. Her family was full of corruption. But I had so much fun with them, drinking beer and wine, smoking weed, and after making several trips moving drugs from Detroit and Dayton, began blowing cocaine. By the time I turned nineteen, my name became well connected with my family's reputation.

Some days when I looked into the mirror, I was ashamed of the person I had become. There was nothing to brag about when the truth behind all our fortune and fame created death traps. Family members were always going to jail, or in and out of drug rehabilitation centers. Meanwhile some of our babies were being separated from their parents, due to the life-threatening environment.

Having my children in my life was truly a blessing, but I realized that I allowed self-pity to victimize them. They grew up around circumstances not intended for any child. I exposed them to an upbringing that even I longed to stay away from.

Superficially, I maintained the luxury of a well-kept family, while the core of my being fed upon the gloom of pity.

Learning to deal with my issues was just what I needed to help me see how a person can appear to be wholesome and successful in the eyes of the public and, at the same time, be a private failure. Losing touch with the Spirit of Righteousness became the biggest of my tragedies. I did everything I could to make others happy, but in reality, I was afraid to face that person in the mirror. I was so far away from that righteous woman, I saw a person of failure.

The expensive clothes my children and I wore came from boosters. The Gucci, Prada, Louis Vuitton, Burberry, and Movado jewelry, etc. came from conning men out of money. I never wanted anyone stealing from me or conning me out of my money, but as it is written, "You reap what you sow." I lost the best years of my life, having children out of wedlock with no desire to be married. My mind was so off balance, and I was so far away from accomplishing my dreams.

The Spirit of Healing provided medical revelations—Even the ungrateful receive from the Giver of Mercy. My neglect over the issue of excessive bleeding during my feminine cycle resulted in my having a hormonal breakdown. During my annual physical, The Spirit of Healing revealed I had fibroids. My attempt at using birth control pills to reduce the cyst on my ovaries seemed to have backfired and caused more harm to my body. My blood level had reached a point that was life-threatening, and I was prescribed medication to restore my iron.

But issues had not turned for the better. My excessive loss of blood nearly became fatal. An emergency surgery to remove my uterus was required. After praying over the matter, I could only trust the Spirit of God to restore my health, along with my faith.

My first priority after having a successful surgery was to live for God's divine purpose. I knew God had been good to me. Being a survivor of such a deadly encounter compelled me to work out and eat healthier. The Spirit of God gave me the tools necessary to regain control over my life and maintain good health. I subdued the fears of past hurt, guilt, and shame by uncovering the challenges of my own issues.

Have you experienced life-changing issues that caused you to bury them inside, from hurt and shame? Take this time to evaluate yourself. Is covering up your experiences strengthening you?

_____

_____

_____

_____

_____

_____

_____

_____

_____

_____

"Behold, we count them happy which endure. Ye have heard of the patience of Job, and have seen the end of the Lord; that the Lord is very pitiful, and of tender mercy" (James 5:11 KJV).

NOTES

Chapter 9

EQUIPPED FOR WAR BECAUSE OF IT

My whole life had dramatically changed and was rearranged when I chose to become a foster parent to girls from newborn through eighteen. I was thirty-eight years old; Brook was seventeen, and LeShawn was twelve. We were very excited about the idea of sharing our home to help other girls. I had made many sacrifices for my girls, so seeing them happy brought my heart a lot of joy. I addressed all the girls as my daughters, and they had no problem with Brook and LeShawn calling them sisters.

I never wanted any girl to come into my home thinking as if I was trying to fulfill the identity of their biological parents. I wanted for them to find in me a maternal sense of comfort, and utilize my shoulders to lean upon, as a cushion to soften any emotional pain.

I spent many sleepless nights in my prayer closet supplicating to The Most High God to give me strength. It was all I could do to keep from breaking down after hearing some of the heartbreaking circumstances my girls had endured. I tried my best to administer enormous amounts of affection and encouragement to them, yet it often wasn't enough for them to feel safe or secure. I believed that I was effective in this service calling, when girls who were disruptive to care in several detention and group homes eagerly chose to live within mine.

Being a foster parent is not an easy task, by no means. On any given day a foster parent's experience may escalate from being cursed out, to lovingly praised, falsely accused, physically attacked, or emotionally attached. I endured disrespect from my teenage girls a lot, especially when they rejected my house rules. My house has been damaged, and repaired. Also, it has been a place where girls ran from and to.

Yet, I couldn't give up on God. After all, those sleepless nights didn't last forever and my tolerance of their behavior helped them understand God's love for them through me.

Several promiscuous young girls ran away from my home. They had stayed with me long enough to get cleaned up, but then they were back on the street. They were addicted to the lifestyle of the streets. I feared for them because I remembered the awful tribulations I faced running away from home after high school graduation. Although, I was equipped with a car and a job, eighteen was too young to be combating the streets. My mind was spiritually dismantled as I was obsessed to embark upon worldly pursuits. I had lost my grip of hope. It was easy for men to violate me. Where was my identity?

I saw that same mentality in the teenagers that ran away.

I instantly identified the girls with the same depleted morals that had me yielding to corruption, sleeping indiscriminately with different men, for cash to buy nice things. No matter how much stuff I acquired, I always found myself left with a broken heart and feeling lonely. Men were comfortable not using condoms, but conceiving a child was not what they wanted.

I was emotionally challenged at crossroads in my young adult life, because I had no satisfactory understanding as to why things happened to me as a child. That's why I was eager to listen, and compassionate with teenage girls who discussed abuse they suffered as a child.

I was very selective when sharing my story with the girls, because they were not mature enough to understand. For a long time, I continued in a downward spiral until the Spirit of Forgiveness taught me how to forgive myself and transcend the pit of brokenness. I had to accept that a lot of things I encountered came from my free will.

I remained prayerful over the hearts and minds of those with a history of running away. Of course it hurts being rejected by my girls, yet I slept at night knowing I had fulfilled my purpose and I found rest in the Lord.

Most of the girls were like my younger self, not knowing how to give, receive, or demonstrate love and compassion. They were used to rejection, feeling unloved, and having an unstable life. But I, myself, had faced many manifestations of chaos, confusion, and torment. Being able to provide a safety net for my girls lifted up my spirit, and helped me realize the true power of forgiveness.

*

With all the challenges I faced with my foster children, I struggled for a long time through mixed emotions trying to find happiness when Brook made me a grandmother at age forty. It finally hit me that my biological girls were facing issues and feelings of being unloved and not having a stable life. I realized that my lack of understanding of personal issues caused a lack in me seeing my children's pain. I didn't know how to accept Brook's pregnancy.

As usual, I blamed myself for her getting pregnant and didn't see what God was doing in our lives. Easily and steadily, The Most High was getting us through this. Amen!

Six months later, I was exposed to the naked truth that I must have faith in The Most High, no matter what. Brook was pregnant again!

It was during this time that I realized healing from my issues was inevitable. I didn't know I had so many issues. My issues had piled up and caused me to make so many bad choices in life, which were part of the struggles I'd faced having my first child. I had to redress the feelings of favor received from The Most High, which empowered my walk away from an empty life with a man ensnared by the use of crack cocaine.

The feeling of distress experienced from past iniquities was slowly resurfacing. I was emotionally messed up and had no control over situations I had blocked out for seventeen years.

My conscience left me to doubt my blessed deliverance and survival over Ced's physical trespass. He was my boyfriend, but that didn't suspend my right to say no. Ced dragged me into my bedroom and raped me, while two-year-old Brook cried herself to sleep. The silence concerning the matter became loud, but being raped would no longer be hush-hush.

As I opened my mind to deal with it, it seemed as if he and I shouted out conspiracy against myself. I had to confess to myself it was a strong possibility of Ced being a part of Brook's DNA. That meant he too shared a part of my grandchildren's DNA.

Was I fixed wholeheartedly, meaning mentally and physically? Did I do the right thing, blocking the pain of being raped out of my mind? Why should I forgive him?

Slowly, roadblocks from my past were being removed as the crime of Ced's sexual assault came to my mind. No one had told me about his addiction to drugs before we met. I had supplied him with cocaine when we started dating, which had slowly crippled him with his daily tasks. Using him for a ride in his nice car and going swimming at the home he shared with his sister were my only intentions. We had sex one time. I had no intentions of establishing a relationship with him. I ended my charade with him that day.

A few weeks passed, and I was in a relationship with Jimmy. I found out I was pregnant weeks later. Jimmy questioned whether he was the father when news got out that I was pregnant. Saying yes seemed like the right thing to say, but I knew it was a toss-up between him and Ced. We stayed together for a few months while I was pregnant. Those were the happiest times of my life. When we broke up, I thought I would be contented with raising my baby alone, but I could never get away from having a boyfriend.

I met this guy name Brandon when I was six months pregnant. He was ready to take on the responsibility of raising my child as a father. I had never met anyone kinder than he. But due to my mood swings and disappearing acts, Brandon called it off a few weeks before my delivery. He argued with me, thinking I had been secretly seeing my baby's father.

The possibility of Ced being the father may have been greater than Jimmy. So when the time came to deliver my baby, I called

Ced to be there with me. A few weeks later, I found a nice two-bedroom house for rent. Since Ced had a legitimate job, I decided to move him in to help with the bills. I was hoping he would make a nice father. His true colors showed when I had to run errands. If it rained or snowed, he would say, "Take your baby with you." Thank you, Jesus. What I thought was a curse was a blessing.

No matter how hard I tried to have a relationship with Ced, feelings for Brandon overpowered me. I invited Brandon to my house several times while Ced was at work. Yes, I did get busted! I'd never expected Ced to get fired from his job. The doorbell rang, Ced opened the door, and Brandon politely asked for me. I played if off as if Brandon was my cousin, and he eventually got the hint to leave. Of course, my affair with Brandon ended that day.

With that being said, how could I not think being beaten and raped was partially my fault? Why did I think it couldn't happen to me? After all, I had seen this type of treatment my whole life. But I didn't hear anyone talk about being raped by their boyfriend.

Ced raped me! He forced me to have sex with him. My screaming and yelling became non-existent. My thoughts were not to awaken my two-year-old daughter, who'd cried herself to sleep after he tossed her in the crib, in the bedroom next to ours. I lay in that bed and took what little more pain he had to give me. I saw in his eyes that even he was getting tired from torturing me, but the anger toward me not supporting his drug habit had more control.

Being beat so badly and dragged from room to room wasn't what hurt me the most. I didn't feel defeated when he punched on me. What I experienced during the rape was worse than anything imaginable. My soul had been ripped from me, and my spirit was broken. Ced forced me to do something I never would have done.

He said, "I know you're going to leave me, so before you go, you're going to suck my penis."

Why should he get that added satisfaction? I asked God to help me. I wanted him to stop. The struggle I had in me wasn't strong enough to keep it from happening. He had his way with me, and no one protected me.

My cousin came to visit me, and we cried together, while I told her that Ced beat and raped me. The next day, I packed up as much as I could and moved in with my mother.

A few weeks later, I got a phone call from Jimmy asking to see his baby. I advised him to get a blood test so we all would know the truth.

We went to the hospital lab to get the blood test, but Jimmy refused to give his DNA. He was already prepared to take on the role of a father. I didn't argue with him when he said, "Let's go."

And we drove away from the lab, with him excited to introduce his daughter to everyone he met.

My family questioned the decision I made to acknowledge Jimmy as my daughter's father, yet Ced never made himself available to challenge my decision. Ced lived a few houses from my aunt, and never once did he try to visit my daughter or ask about her, so the decision I made was final.

Jimmy and his family raised Brook, while I ventured into a world full of corruption. I hooked up with a drug dealer, and when he went to jail, I hooked up with a more notorious drug dealer. During that time I gave birth to another little girl named LeShawn, and took guardianship of my nephew Jigga.

I eventually got sick and tired of that fast lifestyle and moved back to Ohio. Jimmy's heart was broken. He warned me not to leave and threatened to cut all ties with me, which included disassociating himself from his six-year-old little girl, Brook.

My family and I made many attempts to reach out to Ced and his family after I heard about death threats from Dominican drug dealers affiliated with my family. My life and my children's life could have been in danger. I thought it would be wise for Brook to know the possibility of Ced being her father. Brook finally had an opportunity to meet Ced and his family when she turned twelve, and after that, Ced disappeared.

It was very difficult for me to reach out to Ced when Brook had her baby. I kept having flashbacks of the way he had lashed out to hit me when I told him Jimmy raised Brook as his daughter. I didn't want to think about the possibility of him being my daughter's father. The Spirit of Truth wouldn't allow the horrific secret of Ced's rape to rest quietly in my heart in order to protect Brook and others, or myself, from shame.

I wanted to believe I had gotten past all that mess by doing what God wanted me to do. But those memories resurfaced when Brook had her second child, and all I could do was write about it. I wasn't healed from the pain, and there was no getting around it. The Spirit opened a door for me to cross out of the chaos. I had to stop running. The Spirit of Truth put me under arrest. What was once dormant began to erupt inside and became unbearable. Yet I put my trust in the Spirit of Truth and believed it would stand by me. I was no longer free to hide. God fixed me through prayer and fasting.

When the time came for me to address those circumstances with my daughter, it wasn't the best outcome. I accepted the fact that most things cannot be fixed if you leave them unattended. Freeing myself from shame and guilt was what I needed to release. Then I was able to forgive Ced; I no longer needed his apology.

I faced more spiritual dilemmas as I committed to live righteously. The news about LeShawn being pregnant caught me totally off guard. By no means was she ready, nor was I, to raise a baby.

I went from a woman of faith to a woman of fear. I sat in the doctor's office and took a few deep breaths and prayed, "Father God, please destroy my anger, and keep my seventeen-year-old daughter and my grandchild safe during her pregnancy." I put all my trust in the Spirit of God during that time.

LeShawn took online classes and completed all her credits. She graduated from high school and received a scholarship, blowing kisses at her five-month-old baby during her ceremony.

After many years of service, attacks from the enemy continue to follow me, no matter how committed I am to worshiping God. Being a grandmother has been a stormy season for me. LeShawn's father died when she was sixteen, and I can't help thinking how much he would have adored his granddaughter. I often wanted to share the same joy with Brook's father, yet it was very difficult because that meant I had to address my past and Brook's origin.

This is a very touchy part of my life. I took Brook away from Jimmy during the years she really needed his guidance, and I lived in fear of Ced being her biological father. I prayed at night and cried out to the Lord to protect my children and my granddaughters.

Having a relationship with the Spirit changed my view of the world and helped me to stop crying the way I used to. Studying scriptures better equipped me to handle most difficult issues. I didn't back down from believing what's right. Now I am able to address negative opinions in a more positive way.

"And I will rejoice in Jerusalem, and joy in my people: and the voice of weeping shall be no more heard in her, nor the voice of crying" (Isaiah 65:19 NKJV).

Seeing all three of my granddaughters made me realize a woman does not have to possess a queen's ransom to be considered wealthy. I learned the benefits of being wealthy are promoted through finances, eating healthy, living righteously, and being able to enjoy life.

Do you agree that what happens in the dark does come to light? There is always room for improvement. Find a way to right your wrong. What things have you learned to do in a new way?

_____

_____

_____

_____

_____

_____

_____

_____

_____

_____

_____

_____

_____

"He will turn again, he will have compassion upon us; he will subdue our iniquities; and thou wilt cast all their sins into the depths of the sea" (Micah 7:19 KJV).

ALISA D. BOYD

NOTES

Chapter 10

BEING RESTORED FROM IT

I have made many mistakes in my life. I have done things that I know I shouldn't have done. I have said things I shouldn't have said. I have gone places I shouldn't have gone. I have had things in my possession that I shouldn't have had.

But that's not all. It's not always about actions in which I have wrongly participated. What is equally wrong and sinful are some things that I did not do. This included things I should have done, but chose not to, and things I heard said that I knew was wrong but chose not to correct. Also, there were places I should have gone but went elsewhere.

Additionally, it is not always about what I have done or not done. I have come to realize that it's not always about me. I have been around people I should not have been around; sometimes these people may have been responsible for leading me down the wrong path. I would often hear Mother Dear say, "Be careful of the company you keep." Now I truly know what she meant.

I grew up very naïve about other people. Not everyone had my best interest at heart. I had no idea that others would want harm to come to me. This is especially unbelievable when they are members of my own family.

I believed I was powerless as a child. I also believed that a change was needed in my life. I needed more than a superficial, cosmetic change. I needed a change deep down within. Even as a child, I believed I needed restoration.

I learned God is still in the restoration business. He loves me so much and only wants what's best for me. Galatians 6:1 (KJV) states, "Brethren, if a man be overtaken in a fault, ye which are spiritual, restore such an one in the spirit of meekness; considering thyself, lest thou also be tempted."

I often told myself that my behavior was all right when I knew it wasn't. The more I conducted myself in a sinful manner, the easier it was for me to continue in that manner. I had to earnestly ask for forgiveness of my sins before I could receive restoration. And after receiving restoration, I continued to pray to God to keep me living in His will.

Two simple verses helped me understand who I am.

"But ye are a chosen generation, a royal priesthood, an holy nation, a peculiar people; that ye should shew forth the praises of him who hath called you out of the darkness into his marvelous light: Which in time past were not a people, but are now the people of God: which had not obtained mercy, but now have obtained mercy" (1 Peter 2:9-10 KJV).

Receiving restoration from God was just what I personally needed to get past being stuck in a life where I, as well as others around me, was guilty of doing things I should not have been doing. I am so thankful for "Being Restored from It."

It was these very "It-issues" that I had to learn how to handle. I had to learn to release them to The Most High God, who was more than capable of handling them. Once I let go of them, I was free to walk in the purpose that God had for my life.

Today I am able to walk with an identity that represents my interpretation of a faithful relationship with the Spirit of God. I strive each day to live a righteous life by reading scriptures and exercising my faith throughout the week. I admit growing up wasn't easy, but my faith in God has taught me that I can be victorious.

I learned to enjoy life by seeking first the Kingdom of God and His righteousness. The lessons I learned got me through tough seasons and increased my ability to prosper. Today, I live to maintain the imputed righteousness of God in my mind, body, and soul.

I thank the Spirit of God daily for opening doors for me to deal with my issues and give me strength to walk into my destiny.

People of all cultures and creeds have issues, so I am not unique. I confessed my indiscretions and confining issues to help others confront and escape theirs. I hope everyone receives the Good News and personalizes their experience with the Spirit. Here's to a life filled with triumph, humility, compassion, and love for what's righteous and true.

As puzzling as my life has been, I have learned how to overcome obstacles with these two verses:

"Let no one say when he is tempted, I am tempted of God: for God cannot be tempted with evil, neither tempteth he any man. But every man is tempted, when he is drawn away of his own lust, and enticed" (James 1:13-14 KJV).

My thought process goes around in circles, yet I desperately want to take every measure to inspire others to live for the Spirit of Truth. I thank The Most High God for deliverance.

The following elegy **is** inspired from the times I became free to consecrate myself from ungodly deeds in my journey of life.

A SPIRITUAL AWAKENING

You were created with an unknown sight.
I did what I thought was right.
I gave you to your daddy at two years old,
the good, the bad, and the ugly choice
I made to give you a father showed.

I made a dying choice.
A decision made from an undiscerning voice
I messed up; everything was in turmoil.
I sat in a fetal position wanting my embryo.
I couldn't change what I'd already done.
I ached to know that it may have been my son.

I allowed it to happen.
How dare anyone speak words-to abort?
I made a promise-never again.
I regret that day I was beaten.
I cradled my stomach and prayed
my baby's life proceeded.

She said she couldn't love my seed.
That was mine to conceive.
You were my gift from
The Most High God,
I truly believed.

Talks about me were mostly untrue.
I never dated that old man
Her thoughts made me sob.
My life was filled with other sin.
She knew I didn't set him up to be robbed.
She did, bragging about precious gems,
and different men.

Extortion is not my way to stay alive.
I stood at her doorstep and could only say hi.
It crushed me when I told
my children to say bye.
I have a heart; that's how I survived.

I was hurt seeing their heads hung low.
I'm glad I didn't yield to that type of blow.
I was protected from voodoo and witchcraft.
My comrade helped me through the riffraff.

I took heed from the life I almost chose.

I'm delivered with a clear mind that shows.

I understand, Mom, you wanted what's best for me.

I wanted my father to know I really needed him to love me.

I respected the provisions Daddy made for me.

I wish I could have grown up having all my sisters with me.

I wondered was I my brother's only keeper, if so, why me?

I bettered my life when I stopped allowing my family

to dictate for me.

I made it through the pain in a daze.

I was saved by The Most High God's grace.

I sowed a seed and reaped prosperity.

I strive to live righteously now--

that's my reality.

I thank God for allowing me to finally try to "Make Sense of It" as He shared that there is a purpose for the things that happen in my life.

Are you striving today to adopt the spiritual principles that will lead you out of darkness? What part of your purpose in life proclaims praises to The Most High God? Make a mental note of your progress when you put your trust and belief in His voice.

_____

_____

_____

_____

_____

_____

_____

_____

_____

_____

"And the city had no need of the sun, neither of the moon, to shine in it: for the glory of God did lighten it, and the Lamb is the light thereof" (Rev. 21:23 KJV).

Epilogue

What was "it"? In very simple words, "it" refers to my life.

I had to take a good look in the mirror. I asked myself, "Did I address my issues and deal with them the way it appeared the Spirit of God was instructing me?"

The toughest times for me to address was when I was abandoned, lied on, or when I suffered from enormous heartaches and pain.

One of the most crucial mistakes I made as a teenager was trying to deal with issues on my own. Even though the Spirit of The Most High stood by me with every decision I made, anger and pain were always at the center of my thoughts. My problems always seemed to cloud my focus and distorted my vision of life.

The enemy comes in full force. Just when you think you've addressed your issues and everything is okay, the darkest moments surface. Sometimes, you have to dig deep!

The death of my soul came from an unsettling predicament I found myself in at age eighteen that hurt me so bad, after stumbling upon a respected maternal aunt, who had the characteristics of a female pimp. I remembered seeing three men in her apartment dressed in average clothes. A couple weeks later they popped up looking like movie stars. She'd polished them up and turned them out, teaching them how to hustle.

She was always dressed to kill, no matter where she went. I loved her jazzy personality. My aunt having license to do hair and instruct beauty classes was a plus. Thanks to her, most of our family and associates transformed from looking good to looking fabulous from head to toe. She was very compassionate about making people look good. Boosters were always knocking at her door selling clothes, jewelry, and other merchandise.

I walked into adult clubs wearing furs, and dressed fly, thanks to my aunt. Because of my appearance, I was rarely asked for ID. There are not enough words to articulate the positive things I learned from my aunt, who helped me embrace my beauty.

I heard talk in the family about her being a lesbian, but nothing prepared me for the image I witnessed. Seeing my aunt engaging in sex with another woman created a mental breakdown in me. It seemed as though everything I'd known about her being with men was a lie. I saw the way other women treated her for taking their man; I saw her as a real Mac. I didn't know how to process what was going on in my mind.

I made a choice to give up. I just couldn't withstand any more perversions. I told The Most High God I wanted to come live with Christ. At that same time I was thinking, *If there really is a Christ, why am I suffering this way?*

Before swallowing several Excedrin PM pills, I said, "God have mercy on my soul." I walked in a daze up the block with the weight of destruction over my head. I flopped down on the steps of an abandoned building. I had just enough strength to crawl inside my bitter shadow of abandonment.

I looked up and saw bright lights beaming on my face like that of a car losing control, and it appeared to be heading straight toward me. The brightness seemed to envelope me and my entire life as well. I began now to see various dynamics of my experiences from a different perspective.

I was one of the few grandchildren to graduate from high school, but I was too anxious to leave home. I leaped at a grand opportunity for escape. I was hired full-time at my co-op job, and I drove a brand-new car, and yet I used those resources to assist my family with making drug transactions. But I later realized running away to live with my brothers gave no value to my accomplishments. Lost and confused, I walked into an unwholesome environment full of self-pity. But The Spirit of God constantly protected me from many dangers seen and unseen, as I lived with an ungrateful, unappreciative attitude.

A deceitful spirit often told me, "Life would be a lot better if I killed myself." I fought with that spirit for years. But a caring spirit kept telling me, "Don't give up." That whispering sound kept me holding on a little while longer. I could only imagine that it was a protecting angel delegated by the Holy Spirit standing guard to protect me, just like Rev said they do.

No matter what shenanigans were played that day by deceitful spirits to persuade me to end my life, The Most High made them powerless to do so. The Holy Spirit enlivened my fortitude and strengthened me as well as forbade me to take any self-destructive directions. My heart embraced the fact that hell must not be my destination.

A Good Samaritan saw me crying on the stairs and offered me help, and accompanied me through the whole ordeal. He refused to leave until he knew I was okay.

I returned to my aunt's house more enlightened than ever before. Those few pills were not enough to commit suicide, but the idea was more horrific than I'd anticipated. I then promised the delivering Spirit to never go down that road again. What in the world would put me in a state of mind to end my life? Did I really want to die? Did I want to go to hell?

My grandparents' teachings always haunted me. I knew it was wrong for me to participate in unrighteousness. Scriptures of abominations in the Bible from the first two chapters in the book of Romans replayed in my memory. I felt ashamed when I'd witnessed my aunt's passion for another woman. I'd paraded with her friends for so many years, it must have seemed as if I had approved of it.

Even I was eligible for punishment before God for the sins I practiced. I became so overwhelmed with being tuned in to my misery; my best friends were hatred, doubt, and fear. I was tired of bowing down to negative events surfacing around me.

Was that the first time I wanted to commit suicide? Not at all. I learned how to cope with pain, but I didn't know how to deal with stressful feelings of depression. What did I do to overcome my stress and depression? I took medication prescribed by my family doctor for over ten years. Did that help? Not at all. My depression became worse.

My body was immune to prescription pills, so I started smoking cigarettes and drinking wine. The enemy was trying me. But my life was not my own, the Spirit of deliverance was with me all the time. It was a process for me to be delivered from things that had been common to me.

I was a hearer of the Word, but when I became a doer of the laws of righteousness, my dark clouds drew away. I accepted the Word of God in my heart, and reading scriptures brought me so much joy. It was then that I began to understand His will for my life. I detached myself from people, since I no longer wanted to get caught up in what others were doing and what they thought of me. The gauge in my heartbeat changed and was stimulated by happiness and peace.

"My brethren, count it all joy when ye fall into divers temptations" (James 1:2 KJV).

For all the trouble I endured in life, I would not trade the confidence I gained from pursuing a righteous life. I worshiped my King for the knowledge and wisdom He's given me. I'm not perfect by any means, but one thing's for sure—I'm no longer lost in that dark world of corruption. I found my way out, and I chose to have life and to live it more abundantly.

This is only a part of my earthly journey. I have learned by the Grace of God to move on and be strengthened by those years of negative encounters. I am "NOT CREATED TO BREAK!"

Has there ever been a situation in your life that made you feel like giving up? Have you gotten your breakthrough? Take this time to make a difference in your life and understand who you are.

_____

_____

_____

_____

_____

_____

_____

_____

_____

_____

_____

_____

"The righteous cry, and the LORD heareth, and delivereth them out of all their troubles. The LORD is nigh unto them that are of a broken heart; and saveth such as be of a contrite spirit" (Psalms 34:17-18 KJV).

NOTES

Appendix

PRAYING THROUGH IT

I have learned from my many experiences in life that "Prayer Is the Answer," no matter what the question. It doesn't matter what I am going through, how I am feeling about what I'm going through, or even if I am in a position where I feel that I am stuck and not going through at all, I still need to take the time to go to God in prayer. For there is no way that I can go through it without first "Praying Through It."

I can't praise God enough for keeping me through all the bad times, as well as the good. In fact, if it were not for God, I know I wouldn't be here today. Thank you, Lord Jesus.

I present to you, the reader of my book, ten ways I believe God's Will manifested in my life.

Words of Repentance and Appreciation from My Prayer Journal

1. PRAYING FOR LOVE

Thank You, Father, for filling my life with Your love. I thank You for allowing me the opportunity to walk boldly into the blessings You set aside just for me. I know I don't deserve anything You have for me, but I thank You for giving to me in spite of me. Your love is so great that I strive to do whatever I can to please You, for I know beyond the shadow of a doubt that I cannot reach my destiny without You. Amen!

2. PRAYING FOR FORGIVENESS

Thank You, Lord Jesus, for forgiving me. Thank you for teaching me to forgive others, including my family, who for years I blamed for everything bad that happened to me. I blamed them for every bad thought I had, and for every obstacle that came my way. Thank You, God, for opening my eyes to see that I played a major role in everything that happened to me. Help me to know that I must go to and through You for everything. In Jesus' name I pray. Amen!

3. PRAYING FOR HEALING

Dear Lord,

I'm so thankful for having You in my life. I'm thankful for the blood that was shed on the cross for our sins. I ask that You heal the hearts of others that may have been touched from similarities of my history that once caused me pain and confusion. Father, have mercy on the nonbelievers. Father, please heal the minds and souls of men, women, and children who have been deceived from seeing You for who You are as the King of kings and the Lord of Lords. I ask that You permit my faith and anointing to usher in Your glory, so others will see the power You've given me to help at-risk youth. Amen!

4. PRAYING FOR WISDOM

Lord God, I thank You for the wisdom in Your Word. It is when I began to regularly study Your Word that my own wisdom began to increase. I thank You for not only the wisdom You've given me, but for the wisdom You've given my family. Even though I did not recognize it as wisdom during that time, I know now that my grandparents were full of knowledge and wisdom—Your knowledge and wisdom. Lord, I believe Mother Dear kept our family's dark secrets hidden as her way to protect us. She had a blessed assurance that Jesus would supply our every need. Your answer to Mother Dear's prayers bound most evil spirits that crept throughout our nights and wee hours of the morning. Lord, I thank You. Amen!

5. PRAYING FOR FAITH

Lord, I thank You for keeping me safe. I had no clue what was happening to me. I felt so frail and vulnerable. I relied totally on other people's opinions. I bounced around like a ping-pong ball and presented myself as a proud participant in mischievous things with my relatives. I watched different family members take blame for others' mistakes. We had an unspoken rule. We never told on each other. We all stuck together through slick and sin.

Father, I look to You to lead and guide me in the way I should go and protect me from anything that will try to hinder me from reaching my destiny. I ask this in the power of your faith. Amen!

6. PRAYING FOR STRENGTH

Dear God,

You are so amazing. My joyful spirit is lifted every time I think of Your Love when I have no one to turn to, or when all the odds seem to be against me. People have always had their good and bad opinions of me, but because I'm saved, I don't cry the way I used to, or let the opinion of others weigh me down. I'm so grateful for the happiness You have restored in me. My family is not the perfect family, but I appreciate my mother and my father for having me.

My relatives and I are not very close, but I'm thankful for the good conversations You've allowed us to share. I pray that I as well as others have strength to take up our cross and make an everlasting imprint on this world to help edify the building of Your Kingdom. Amen!

7. PRAYING FOR DELIVERANCE

Lord, I thank You for being with me. You were there when I witnessed the dividing spirit of competition wrapping itself around my relatives. You know I hated seeing the gleam in my cousin's eyes when they sinned against You. I thank You, Father, for shielding me from such an evil spirit. Lord, only You know how hard I struggled to fit in with my family. So I thank You for Your deliverance.

Dear Lord Jesus, I admit that I am a sinner, that You died on the cross for my sins, and that You arose again from the grave. I turn away from my sins and invite You to come live in my heart and be Lord of my life. Thank You, Lord Jesus, for forgiving me, for loving me, and for dying for me. Now please help me to live for You and to never be ashamed of You. In Jesus' name I pray. Amen!

8. PRAYING FOR PROTECTION

Father, I thank You for protecting me from many dangers both seen and unseen. You knew beforehand the struggles I would face as I entered into Your gates. Therefore, please help me to be forever humble and always adhere to Your Word and directions.

I thank You for letting me grow up with my grandparents, who desired to protect me. I'm also grateful for Your host of angels that kept me from being destroyed by the horrors transferred through generations of my family. Thank You for the courage to combat demonic spirits that haunt my bloodline. The enemy sought to hold us at its mercy, but Your grace continued to protect us from its destructive assault and all its lies.

Father, You have always been there for me in every situation that seemed almost impossible for me to conquer. Messages of Your word are instilled in me through my grandfather's preaching. Please continue to give me the strength to stand. Amen!

9. PRAYING FOR PEACE

I thank You for Your gift of peace in removing the spirit of fear from my mind and wiping the tears from my eyes.

Father, You know how I wanted to make my grandparents proud by doing what's right. But even when I knowingly did wrong in Your sight, You have forgiven me and given me Your peace. I'm so grateful You led my Sunday school teacher to teach me to respect my body as the Lord's temple. She taught me that sex is a beautiful thing and should be saved for marriage. She encouraged me to stay strong in Your peace.

Rev also taught us that no person or power on earth can destroy a soul that abided in You unless we permitted their negative spirit to break us.

Lord, thank You for Your peace. Amen!

10. PRAYING FOR THE WILL OF GOD TO BE DONE IN MY LIFE

Lord, I thank You for guiding me through the challenges in my life. I thank You for the opportunity to give my life totally to You so that You can do whatever Your will is for me. Have mercy on my soul and let me die from my fleshly desires. Trust me to carry Your word in my heart and do all that You have called me to do. Anoint my eyes, my mind, my heart, and my soul as I venture through the journey of my past, my present, and the possibilities of my future. Thank You. Amen!

Have you learned that you can pray your way through any circumstance in your life? Are you beginning to realize that every circumstance provides you with a worship experience?

_____

_____

_____

_____

_____

_____

_____

_____

_____

"If any of you lack wisdom, let him ask of God, that giveth to all men liberally, and upbraideth not; and it shall be given him. But let him ask in faith, nothing wavering. For he that wavereth is like a wave of the sea driven with the wind and tossed" (James 1:5-6 KJV).

ABOUT THE AUTHOR

Alisa Doreen Boyd was born in Dayton, Ohio. After graduating in 1983 from John H. Patterson Co-op High School, she moved to Detroit, Michigan. She received a CNA and worked in the medical field. Ten years later, she moved back to Dayton, Ohio and received an associate's degree in business management. One of her greatest accomplishments was helping launch a charter school. She was also very active in the community, as well her church.

In 2002, she moved to Atlanta, Georgia. There, she was inspired by her nephew, and received confirmation, after watching a Wednesday Child Special aired on Fox Atlanta News to become a foster parent. She didn't want to adopt, but was licensed to care for three girls. She also maintained a full-time position with DeKalb County Finance Department as senior accounting tech.

She obtained a bachelor's degree in business administration with a concentration in legal studies, graduating magna cum laude from Strayer University.

She is the CEO of Mother Dillard's Village of Hope, a nonprofit organization for at-risk youth, and serves with the Greeters Ministry at New Birth Missionary Baptist Church. She is single, and has never been married. When she's not working, she loves to read, travel, and learn more about the Word of God.

As a young girl, Alisa D. Boyd moved from place to place; room to room, house to house, city to city, state to state. As she became a young woman, she saw a need to revisit her past. She then journeyed through time---tough times, good times, the times of a life filled with pain and glory. Certainly, something was hidden and left behind, waiting to be found by its rightful owner, an owner who would someday search for self-possession and self-completion.

As a young adult, she continued on a diminishing path, losing more and more of less and less of what was left of her. There was an imperfect development, different from what she thought she could be, during those losses, and no gain. Unlike her childhood, some of her was lost to the men she invited into her life---and her bed.

There were, however, three blessings that came during the worst of times: her two beautiful daughters and her nephew. They and the blessed memories of her grandparents became her reason for being, for doing, and for changing her life.

It was her grandparents who'd formally introduced her to God. The memory of their songs and prayers still rings in her ears, and it was that ringing that summoned her back in time and in a place to confront her lifelong issues face to face.

FROM THE AUTHOR

In my journey, which became necessary for my survival, I rediscovered, reclaimed, and repositioned the pieces of me that I had abandoned so many years ago. I renovated those lost pieces of myself and began receiving gifts that God always wanted me to have. With my gifts from God, I defeated my weakness, and I strive to declare victory on a daily basis. I WAS NOT CREATED TO BREAK!

I have made several spiritual connections in my life that I am sure were God-ordained to empower me in my spiritual journey.

As a foster parent and a volunteer for agencies that assist with the hungry and the homeless, I realize there are so many people who get lost on the first level of God's glory, blinded and searching on their own for unity and fullness in a shady world. These people do not know if it is better to fall for God or fall for man. I would like to encourage these people and give them confidence to understand the importance of spiritual guidance in tackling obstacles.

I hope there's a message that will divert people from a premature death as they face encounters on their journey through the valley of the shadow of death. I pray that there is a chapter or a poem that will give understanding that God changes people and their situations. God did not intend for His children to come out empty-handed.

I hope my God-given talent will bring youth under a shield that will allow them to become off limits to the enemy. I have established a nonprofit organization for at-risk youth: **Mother Dillard's Village of Hope (www.mdvh.org)**.

Part of the proceeds from my book will help make this program a reality. Please support me, so together we can establish a residential facility for youth who are homeless, victimized by human trafficking, and at risk. Remember, it takes a village. And most importantly, we are **NOT CREATED TO BREAK!**

Alisa